OpenCV with Python Blueprints

Design and develop advanced computer vision projects using OpenCV with Python

Michael Beyeler

[PACKT]
PUBLISHING

open source*
community experience distilled

BIRMINGHAM - MUMBAI

OpenCV with Python Blueprints

Copyright © 2015 Packt Publishing

First published: October 2015

Production reference: 1141015

Published by Packt Publishing Ltd.
Livery Place
35 Livery Street
Birmingham B3 2PB, UK.

ISBN 978-1-78528-269-0

www.packtpub.com

Credits

Author
Michael Beyeler

Reviewers
Jia-Shen Boon
Florian LE BOURDAIS
Steve Goldsmith
Rahul Kavi
Scott Lobdell
Vipul Sharma

Commissioning Editor
Akram Hussain

Acquisition Editor
Divya Poojari

Content Development Editor
Zeeyan Pinheiro

Technical Editor
Namrata Patil

Copy Editor
Vikrant Phadke

Project Coordinator
Suzanne Coutinho

Proofreader
Safis Editing

Indexer
Rekha Nair

Production Coordinator
Melwyn D'sa

Cover Work
Melwyn D'sa

About the Author

Michael Beyeler is a PhD candidate in the department of computer science at the University of California, Irvine, where he is working on computational models of the brain as well as their integration into autonomous brain-inspired robots. His work on vision-based navigation, learning, and cognition has been presented at IEEE conferences and published in international journals. Currently, he is one of the main developers of CARLsim, an open source GPGPU spiking neural network simulator.

This is his first technical book that, in contrast to his (or any) dissertation, might actually be read.

Michael has professional programming experience in Python, C/C++, CUDA, MATLAB, and Android. Born and raised in Switzerland, he received a BSc degree in electrical engineering and information technology, as well as a MSc degree in biomedical engineering from ETH Zurich. When he is not "nerding out" on robots, he can be found on top of a snowy mountain, in front of a live band, or behind the piano.

I would like to thank Packt Publishing for this great opportunity and their support, my girlfriend for putting up with my late-night writing sessions, as well as the technical reviewers, who have spotted (hopefully) all my glaring errors and helped make this book a success.

About the Reviewers

Jia-Shen Boon is a researcher in robotics at the University of Wisconsin-Madison, supervised by Professor Michael Coen. He is a proud son of the sunny city-state of Singapore. Before coming to Wisconsin, he was a research engineer at DSO National Labs, where he worked on autonomous underwater vehicles and other unspeakable things. During his free time, Jia-Shen likes to study the Japanese language and write about himself in the third person.

Florian LE BOURDAIS hails from France and Germany. While he was growing up in the lazy south of France, an encounter with music from The Beatles gave him an early grasp of the English language. One of his earliest childhood memories has him watching his older German cousin, Dominik, coding a Tetris clone in the family basement using QBasic. High school and the advent of hand-held calculators led him to write his first Snake program using the TI-Basic language. After having acquired a solid background in mathematics and physics, Florian was admitted to one of the top French engineering schools. He studied mechanical engineering, but interned as an index-arbitrage trader in Japan during the financial crisis. Keen to come back to a country he much liked, he specialized in nuclear engineering and was doing an internship in a Japanese fast-breeder reactor during the Fukushima nuclear crisis.

Coming back to France, Florian was happy to start an engineering job in non-destructive testing. He specializes in ultrasound inspection methods, with a focus on phased array transducers, guided waves, and EMATs. He has published more than 10 international conference proceedings. At night, he's a hacker who likes to play with 3D printers, fermented Korean cabbage, the Raspberry Pi, Japanese characters, and guitars. He regularly writes a blog about his side projects at `http://flothesof.github.io`.

I would like to thank my friends and family for supporting me throughout this project. Special thanks goes to my favorite machine learning specialists at the Geeks d'Orléans, as well as Coloc du 1000.

Rahul Kavi is a PhD student at West Virginia University. He holds a master's degree in computer science. He is pursuing a PhD in the area of distributed machine learning and computer vision. He is a computer vision and robotics enthusiast. Rahul has worked on developing prototypes, optimizing computer vision, and machine learning applications for desktops, mobile devices, and autonomous robots. He writes blogs on his research interests and part-time projects at `www.developerstation.org`. He is a source code contributor to OpenCV.

Vipul Sharma is an engineering undergraduate from Jabalpur Engineering College. He is an ardent Python enthusiast and was one of the students selected for Google Summer of Code 2015 under the Python Software Foundation. He has been actively involved in Python and OpenCV since 2012. A few of his projects on OpenCV include a motion sensing surveillance camera, hand-gesture recognition, and solving a Rubik's cube by reading images of its faces in real time. Vipul loves contributing to open source software and is currently working on Optical Character Recognition (OCR) using OpenCV. You can check out his projects at `https://github.com/vipul-sharma20`.

www.PacktPub.com

Support files, eBooks, discount offers, and more

For support files and downloads related to your book, please visit www.PacktPub.com.

Did you know that Packt offers eBook versions of every book published, with PDF and ePub files available? You can upgrade to the eBook version at www.PacktPub.com and as a print book customer, you are entitled to a discount on the eBook copy. Get in touch with us at service@packtpub.com for more details.

At www.PacktPub.com, you can also read a collection of free technical articles, sign up for a range of free newsletters and receive exclusive discounts and offers on Packt books and eBooks.

https://www2.packtpub.com/books/subscription/packtlib

Do you need instant solutions to your IT questions? PacktLib is Packt's online digital book library. Here, you can search, access, and read Packt's entire library of books.

Why subscribe?

- Fully searchable across every book published by Packt
- Copy and paste, print, and bookmark content
- On demand and accessible via a web browser

Free access for Packt account holders

If you have an account with Packt at www.PacktPub.com, you can use this to access PacktLib today and view 9 entirely free books. Simply use your login credentials for immediate access.

Table of Contents

Preface

OpenCV is a native, cross-platform C++ library for computer vision, machine learning, and image processing. It is increasingly being adopted in Python for development. OpenCV has C++/C, Python, and Java interfaces, with support for Windows, Linux, Mac, iOS, and Android. Developers who use OpenCV build applications to process visual data; this can include live streaming data such as photographs or videos from a device such as a camera. However, as developers move beyond their first computer vision applications, they might find it difficult to come up with solutions that are well-optimized, robust, and scalable for real-world scenarios.

This book demonstrates how to develop a series of intermediate to advanced projects using OpenCV and Python, rather than teaching the core concepts of OpenCV in theoretical lessons. The working projects developed in this book teach you how to apply your theoretical knowledge to topics such as image manipulation, augmented reality, object tracking, 3D scene reconstruction, statistical learning, and object categorization.

By the end of this book, you will be an OpenCV expert, and your newly gained experience will allow you to develop your own advanced computer vision applications.

What this book covers

Chapter 1, *Fun with Filters*, explores a number of interesting image filters (such as a black-and-white pencil sketch, warming/cooling filters, and a cartoonizer effect), and we apply them to the video stream of a webcam in real time.

Chapter 2, *Hand Gesture Recognition Using a Kinect Depth Sensor*, helps you develop an app to detect and track simple hand gestures in real time using the output of a depth sensor, such as a Microsoft Kinect 3D Sensor or Asus Xtion.

Chapter 3, Finding Objects via Feature Matching and Perspective Transforms, is where you develop an app to detect an arbitrary object of interest in the video stream of a webcam, even if the object is viewed from different angles or distances, or under partial occlusion.

Chapter 4, 3D Scene Reconstruction Using Structure from Motion, shows you how to reconstruct and visualize a scene in 3D by inferring its geometrical features from camera motion.

Chapter 5, Tracking Visually Salient Objects, helps you develop an app to track multiple visually salient objects in a video sequence (such as all the players on the field during a soccer match) at once.

Chapter 6, Learning to Recognize Traffic Signs, shows you how to train a support vector machine to recognize traffic signs from the German Traffic Sign Recognition Benchmark (GTSRB) dataset.

Chapter 7, Learning to Recognize Emotions on Faces, is where you develop an app that is able to both detect faces and recognize their emotional expressions in the video stream of a webcam in real time.

What you need for this book

This book supports several operating systems as development environments, including Windows XP or a later version, Max OS X 10.6 or a later version, and Ubuntu12.04 or a later version. The only hardware requirement is a webcam (or camera device), except for in *Chapter 2, Hand Gesture Recognition Using a Kinect Depth Sensor*, which instead requires access to a Microsoft Kinect 3D Sensor or an Asus Xtion.

The book contains seven projects, with the following requirements.

All projects can run on any of Windows, Mac, or Linux, and they require the following software packages:

- **OpenCV** 2.4.9 or later: Recent 32-bit and 64-bit versions as well as installation instructions are available at http://opencv.org/downloads. html. Platform-specific installation instructions can be found at http:// docs.opencv.org/doc/tutorials/introduction/table_of_content_ introduction/table_of_content_introduction.html.

- **Python** 2.7 or later: Recent 32-bit and 64-bit installers are available at https://www.python.org/downloads. The installation instructions can be found at https://wiki.python.org/moin/BeginnersGuide/Download.

- **NumPy** 1.9.2 or later: This package for scientific computing officially comes in 32-bit format only, and can be obtained from `http://www.scipy.org/scipylib/download.html`. The installation instructions can be found at `http://www.scipy.org/scipylib/building/index.html#building`.

- **wxPython** 2.8 or later: This GUI programming toolkit can be obtained from `http://www.wxpython.org/download.php`. Its installation instructions are given at `http://wxpython.org/builddoc.php`.

In addition, some chapters require the following free Python modules:

- **SciPy** 0.16.0 or later (Chapter 1): This scientific Python library officially comes in 32-bit only, and can be obtained from `http://www.scipy.org/scipylib/download.html`. The installation instructions can be found at `http://www.scipy.org/scipylib/building/index.html#building`.

- **matplotlib** 1.4.3 or later (Chapters 4 to 7): This 2D plotting library can be obtained from `http://matplotlib.org/downloads.html`. Its installation instructions can be found by going to `http://matplotlib.org/faq/installing_faq.html#how-to-install`.

- **libfreenect** 0.5.2 or later (Chapter 2): The libfreenect module by the OpenKinect project (`http://www.openkinect.org`) provides drivers and libraries for the Microsoft Kinect hardware, and can be obtained from `https://github.com/OpenKinect/libfreenect`. Its installation instructions can be found at `http://openkinect.org/wiki/Getting_Started`.

Furthermore, the use of **iPython** (`http://ipython.org/install.html`) is highly recommended as it provides a flexible, interactive console interface.

Finally, if you are looking for help or get stuck along the way, you can go to several websites that provide excellent help, documentation, and tutorials:

- The official OpenCV API reference, user guide, and tutorials: `http://docs.opencv.org`

- The official OpenCV forum: `http://www.answers.opencv.org/questions`

- OpenCV-Python tutorials by Alexander Mordvintsev and Abid Rahman K: `http://opencv-python-tutroals.readthedocs.org/en/latest`

Who this book is for

This book is for intermediate users of OpenCV who aim to master their skills by developing advanced practical applications. You should already have some experience of building simple applications, and you are expected to be familiar with OpenCV's concepts and Python libraries. Basic knowledge of Python programming is expected and assumed.

Conventions

In this book, you will find a number of styles of text that distinguish between different kinds of information. Here are some examples of these styles, and an explanation of their meaning.

Code words in text, database table names, folder names, filenames, file extensions, pathnames, dummy URLs, user input, and Twitter handles are shown as follows: "In OpenCV, a webcam can be accessed with a call to `cv2.VideoCapture`."

A block of code is set as follows:

```
def main():
    capture = cv2.VideoCapture(0)
    if not(capture.isOpened()):
        capture.open()
    capture.set(cv2.cv.CV_CAP_PROP_FRAME_WIDTH, 640)
    capture.set(cv2.cv.CV_CAP_PROP_FRAME_HEIGHT, 480)
```

New terms and **important words** are shown in bold. Words that you see on the screen, in menus or dialog boxes for example, appear in the text like this: "The **Take Snapshot** button is placed below the radio buttons."

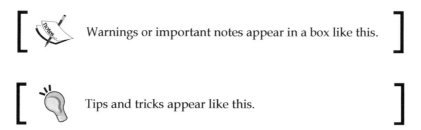

Warnings or important notes appear in a box like this.

Tips and tricks appear like this.

Reader feedback

Feedback from our readers is always welcome. Let us know what you think about this book—what you liked or may have disliked. Reader feedback is important for us to develop titles that you really get the most out of.

To send us general feedback, simply send an e-mail to feedback@packtpub.com, and mention the book title via the subject of your message.

If there is a topic that you have expertise in and you are interested in either writing or contributing to a book, see our author guide on www.packtpub.com/authors.

Customer support

Now that you are the proud owner of a Packt book, we have a number of things to help you to get the most from your purchase.

Downloading the example code

You can download the example code files for all Packt books you have purchased from your account at http://www.packtpub.com. If you purchased this book elsewhere, you can visit http://www.packtpub.com/support and register to have the files e-mailed directly to you. The latest and most up-to-date example code for this book is also publicly available on GitHub: http://www.github.com/mbeyeler/opencv-python-blueprints.

Downloading the color images of this book

We also provide you with a PDF file that has color images of the screenshots/diagrams used in this book. The color images will help you better understand the changes in the output. You can download this file from https://www.packtpub.com/sites/default/files/downloads/OpenCVwithPythonBlueprints_ColorImages.pdf.

Errata

Although we have taken every care to ensure the accuracy of our content, mistakes do happen. If you find a mistake in one of our books—maybe a mistake in the text or the code—we would be grateful if you would report this to us. By doing so, you can save other readers from frustration and help us improve subsequent versions of this book. If you find any errata, please report them by visiting http://www.packtpub. com/submit-errata, selecting your book, clicking on the **errata submission form** link, and entering the details of your errata. Once your errata are verified, your submission will be accepted and the errata will be uploaded on our website, or added to any list of existing errata, under the Errata section of that title. Any existing errata can be viewed by selecting your title from http://www.packtpub.com/support.

Piracy

Piracy of copyright material on the Internet is an ongoing problem across all media. At Packt, we take the protection of our copyright and licenses very seriously. If you come across any illegal copies of our works, in any form, on the Internet, please provide us with the location address or website name immediately so that we can pursue a remedy.

Please contact us at copyright@packtpub.com with a link to the suspected pirated material.

We appreciate your help in protecting our authors and our ability to bring you valuable content.

Questions

You can contact us at questions@packtpub.com if you are having a problem with any aspect of the book, and we will do our best to address it.

1
Fun with Filters

The goal of this chapter is to develop a number of image processing filters and apply them to the video stream of a webcam in real time. These filters will rely on various OpenCV functions to manipulate matrices through splitting, merging, arithmetic operations, and applying lookup tables for complex functions.

The three effects are as follows:

- **Black-and-white pencil sketch**: To create this effect, we will make use of two image blending techniques, known as **dodging** and **burning**
- **Warming/cooling filters**: To create these effects, we will implement our own **curve filters** using a lookup table
- **Cartoonizer**: To create this effect, we will combine a **bilateral filter**, a **median filter**, and **adaptive thresholding**

OpenCV is such an advanced toolchain that often the question is not how to implement something from scratch, but rather which pre-canned implementation to choose for your needs. Generating complex effects is not hard if you have a lot of computing resources to spare. The challenge usually lies in finding an approach that not only gets the job done, but also gets it done in time.

Instead of teaching the basic concepts of image manipulation through theoretical lessons, we will take a practical approach and develop a single end-to-end app that integrates a number of image filtering techniques. We will apply our theoretical knowledge to arrive at a solution that not only works but also speeds up seemingly complex effects so that a laptop can produce them in real time.

The following screenshot shows the final outcome of the three effects running on a laptop:

 All of the code in this book is targeted for OpenCV 2.4.9 and has been tested on Ubuntu 14.04. Throughout this book, we will make extensive use of the NumPy package (http://www.numpy.org). In addition, this chapter requires the UnivariateSpline module of the SciPy package (http://www.scipy.org) as well as the wxPython 2.8 graphical user interface (http://www.wxpython.org/download. php) for cross-platform GUI applications. We will try to avoid further dependencies wherever possible.

Planning the app

The final app will consist of the following modules and scripts:

- `filters`: A module comprising different classes for the three different image effects. The modular approach will allow us to use the filters independently of any **graphical user interface** (**GUI**).

- `filters.PencilSketch`: A class for applying the pencil sketch effect to an RGB color image.

- `filters.WarmingFilter`: A class for applying the warming filter to an RGB color image.

- `filters.CoolingFilter`: A class for applying the cooling filter to an RGB color image.

- `filters.Cartoonizer`: A method for applying the cartoonizer effect to an RGB color image.

- `gui`: A module that provides a wxPython GUI application to access the webcam and display the camera feed, which we will make extensive use of throughout the book.

- `gui.BaseLayout`: A generic layout from which more complicated layouts can be built.

- `chapter1`: The main script for this chapter.

- `chapter1.FilterLayout`: A custom layout based on `gui.BaseLayout` that displays the camera feed and a row of radio buttons that allows the user to select from the available image filters to be applied to each frame of the camera feed.

- `chapter1.main`: The main function routine for starting the GUI application and accessing the webcam.

Creating a black-and-white pencil sketch

In order to obtain a pencil sketch (that is, a black-and-white drawing) of the camera frame, we will make use of two image blending techniques, known as **dodging** and **burning**. These terms refer to techniques employed during the printing process in traditional photography; photographers would manipulate the exposure time of a certain area of a darkroom print in order to lighten or darken it. Dodging lightens an image, whereas burning darkens it.

Areas that were not supposed to undergo changes were protected with a **mask**. Today, modern image editing programs, such as Photoshop and Gimp, offer ways to mimic these effects in digital images. For example, masks are still used to mimic the effect of changing exposure time of an image, wherein areas of a mask with relatively intense values will *expose* the image more, thus lightening the image. OpenCV does not offer a native function to implement these techniques, but with a little insight and a few tricks, we will arrive at our own efficient implementation that can be used to produce a beautiful pencil sketch effect.

If you search on the Internet, you might stumble upon the following common procedure to achieve a pencil sketch from an RGB color image:

1. Convert the color image to grayscale.

2. Invert the grayscale image to get a negative.

3. Apply a Gaussian blur to the negative from step 2.

4. Blend the grayscale image from step 1 with the blurred negative from step 3 using a color dodge.

Whereas steps 1 to 3 are straightforward, step 4 can be a little tricky. Let's get that one out of the way first.

> OpenCV 3 comes with a pencil sketch effect right out of the box. The cv2.pencilSketch function uses a domain filter introduced in the 2011 paper *Domain transform for edge-aware image and video processing*, by Eduardo Gastal and Manuel Oliveira. However, for the purpose of this book, we will develop our own filter.

Implementing dodging and burning in OpenCV

In modern image editing tools, such as Photoshop, color dodging of an image A with a mask B is implemented as the following ternary statement acting on every pixel index, called idx:

```
((B[idx] == 255) ? B[idx] :
    min(255, ((A[idx] << 8) / (255-B[idx])))))
```

This essentially divides the value of an A[idx] image pixel by the inverse of the B[idx] mask pixel value, while making sure that the resulting pixel value will be in the range of [0, 255] and that we do not divide by zero.

We could translate this into the following naïve Python function, which accepts two OpenCV matrices (image and mask) and returns the blended image:

```
def dodgeNaive(image, mask):
    # determine the shape of the input image
    width,height = image.shape[:2]

    # prepare output argument with same size as image
    blend = np.zeros((width,height), np.uint8)

    for col in xrange(width):
        for row in xrange(height):

            # shift image pixel value by 8 bits
            # divide by the inverse of the mask
            tmp = (image[c,r] << 8) / (255.-mask)

            # make sure resulting value stays within bounds
            if tmp > 255:
                tmp = 255
            blend[c,r] = tmp
    return blend
```

As you might have guessed, although this code might be functionally correct, it will undoubtedly be horrendously slow. Firstly, the function uses for loops, which are almost always a bad idea in Python. Secondly, NumPy arrays (the underlying format of OpenCV images in Python) are optimized for array calculations, so accessing and modifying each image[c,r] pixel separately will be really slow.

Instead, we should realize that the <<8 operation is the same as multiplying the pixel value with the number $2^8=256$, and that pixel-wise division can be achieved with the cv2.divide function. Thus, an improved version of our dodge function could look like this:

```
import cv2

def dodgeV2(image, mask):
    return cv2.divide(image, 255-mask, scale=256)
```

We have reduced the dodge function to a single line! The dodgeV2 function produces the same result as dodgeNaive but is orders of magnitude faster. In addition, cv2.divide automatically takes care of division by zero, making the result 0 where 255-mask is zero.

Now, it is straightforward to implement an analogous burning function, which divides the inverted image by the inverted mask and inverts the result:

```
import cv2

def burnV2(image, mask):
    return 255 - cv2.divide(255-image, 255-mask, scale=256)
```

Pencil sketch transformation

With these tricks in our bag, we are now ready to take a look at the entire procedure. The final code will be in its own class in the `filters` module. After we have converted a color image to grayscale, we aim to blend this image with its blurred negative:

1. We import the OpenCV and `numpy` modules:

    ```
    import cv2
    import numpy as np
    ```

2. Instantiate the `PencilSketch` class:

    ```
    class PencilSketch:
        def __init__(self, (width, height),
            bg_gray='pencilsketch_bg.jpg'):
    ```

    The constructor of this class will accept the image dimensions as well as an optional background image, which we will make use of in just a bit. If the file exists, we will open it and scale it to the right size:

    ```
    self.width = width
    self.height = height

    # try to open background canvas (if it exists)
    self.canvas = cv2.imread(bg_gray, cv2.CV_8UC1)
    if self.canvas is not None:
        self.canvas = cv2.resize(self.canvas,
            (self.width, self.height))
    ```

3. Add a render method that will perform the pencil sketch:

    ```
    def renderV2(self, img_rgb):
    ```

4. Converting an RGB image (imgRGB) to grayscale is straightforward:

    ```
    img_gray = cv2.cvtColor(img_rgb, cv2.COLOR_RGB2GRAY)
    ```

    Note that it does not matter whether the input image is RGB or BGR.

5. We then invert the image and blur it with a large Gaussian kernel of size (21,21):

```
img_gray_inv = 255 - img_gray
img_blur = cv2.GaussianBlur(img_gray_inv, (21,21), 0, 0)
```

6. We use our dodgeV2 dodging function from the aforementioned code to blend the original grayscale image with the blurred inverse:

```
img_blend = dodgeV2(mg_gray, img_blur)
return cv2.cvtColor(img_blend, cv2.COLOR_GRAY2RGB)
```

The resulting image looks like this:

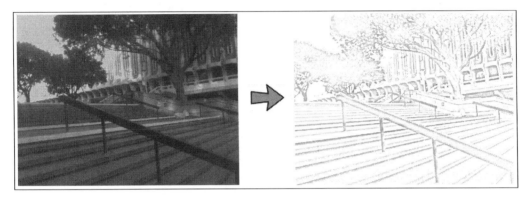

Did you notice that our code can be optimized further?

A Gaussian blur is basically a convolution with a Gaussian function. One of the beauties of convolutions is their associative property. This means that it does not matter whether we first invert the image and then blur it, or first blur the image and then invert it.

"Then what matters?" you might ask. Well, if we start with a blurred image and pass its inverse to the dodgeV2 function, then within that function, the image will get inverted again (the 255-mask part), essentially yielding the original image. If we get rid of these redundant operations, an optimized render method would look like this:

```
def render(img_rgb):
    img_gray = cv2.cvtColor(img_rgb, cv2.COLOR_BGR2GRAY)
    img_blur = cv2.GaussianBlur(img_gray, (21,21), 0, 0)
    img_blend = cv2.divide(img_gray, img_blur, scale=256)
    return img_blend
```

For kicks and giggles, we want to lightly blend our transformed image (`img_blend`) with a background image (`self.canvas`) that makes it look as if we drew the image on a canvas:

```
if self.canvas is not None:
    img_blend = cv2.multiply(img_blend, self.canvas, scale=1./256)
return cv2.cvtColor(img_blend, cv2.COLOR_GRAY2BGR)
```

And we're done! The final output looks like what is shown here:

Generating a warming/cooling filter

When we perceive images, our brain picks up on a number of subtle clues to infer important details about the scene. For example, in broad daylight, highlights may have a slightly yellowish tint because they are in direct sunlight, whereas shadows may appear slightly bluish due to the ambient light of the blue sky. When we view an image with such color properties, we might immediately think of a *sunny day*.

This effect is no mystery to photographers, who sometimes purposely manipulate the white balance of an image to convey a certain mood. Warm colors are generally perceived as more pleasant, whereas cool colors are associated with night and drabness.

To manipulate the perceived **color temperature** of an image, we will implement a **curve filter**. These filters control how color transitions appear between different regions of an image, allowing us to subtly shift the color spectrum without adding an unnatural-looking overall tint to the image.

Color manipulation via curve shifting

A curve filter is essentially a function, $y = f(x)$, that maps an input pixel value x to an output pixel value y. The curve is parameterized by a set of $n+1$ anchor points, as follows: $\{(x\_0, y\_0), (x\_1, y\_1), ..., (x\_n, y\_n)\}$.

Each anchor point is a pair of numbers that represent the input and output pixel values. For example, the pair *(30, 90)* means that an input pixel value of 30 is increased to an output value of 90. Values between anchor points are interpolated along a smooth curve (hence the name curve filter).

Such a filter can be applied to any image channel, be it a single grayscale channel or the R, G, and B channels of an RGB color image. Thus, for our purposes, all values of x and y must stay between 0 and 255.

For example, if we wanted to make a grayscale image slightly brighter, we could use a curve filter with the following set of control points: *{(0,0), (128, 192), (255,255)}*. This would mean that all input pixel values except 0 and 255 would be increased slightly, resulting in an overall brightening effect of the image.

If we want such filters to produce natural-looking images, it is important to respect the following two rules:

- Every set of anchor points should include *(0,0)* and *(255,255)*. This is important in order to prevent the image from appearing as if it has an overall tint, as black remains black and white remains white.

- The function $f(x)$ should be monotonously increasing. In other words, with increasing x, $f(x)$ either stays the same or increases (that is, it never decreases). This important for making sure that shadows remain shadows and highlights remain highlights.

Implementing a curve filter by using lookup tables

Curve filters are computationally expensive, because the values of $f(x)$ must be interpolated whenever x does not coincide with one of the prespecified anchor points. Performing this computation for every pixel of every image frame that we encounter would have dramatic effects on performance.

Instead, we make use of a lookup table. Since there are only 256 possible pixel values for our purposes, we need to calculate *f(x)* only for all the 256 possible values of *x*. Interpolation is handled by the `UnivariateSpline` function of the `scipy.interpolate` module, as shown in the following code snippet:

```
from scipy.interpolate import UnivariateSpline

def _create_LUT_8UC1(self, x, y):
    spl = UnivariateSpline(x, y)
    return spl(xrange(256))
```

The `return` argument of the function is a 256-element list that contains the interpolated *f(x)* values for every possible value of *x*.

All we need to do now is come up with a set of anchor points, *(x_i, y_i)*, and we are ready to apply the filter to a grayscale input image (`img_gray`):

```
import cv2
import numpy as np

x = [0, 128, 255]
y = [0, 192, 255]
myLUT = _create_LUT_8UC1(x, y)
img_curved = cv2.LUT(img_gray, myLUT).astype(np.uint8)
```

The result looks like this (the original image is on the left, and the transformed image is on the right):

Designing the warming/cooling effect

With the mechanism to quickly apply a generic curve filter to any image channel in place, we now turn to the question of how to manipulate the perceived color temperature of an image. Again, the final code will have its own class in the `filters` module.

If you have a minute to spare, I advise you to play around with the different curve settings for a while. You can choose any number of anchor points and apply the curve filter to any image channel you can think of (red, green, blue, hue, saturation, brightness, lightness, and so on). You could even combine multiple channels, or decrease one and shift another to a desired region. What will the result look like?

However, if the number of possibilities dazzles you, take a more conservative approach. First, by making use of our _create_LUT_8UC1 function developed in the preceding steps, let's define two generic curve filters, one that (by trend) increases all pixel values of a channel, and one that generally decreases them:

```
class WarmingFilter:

    def __init__(self):
        self.incr_ch_lut = _create_LUT_8UC1([0, 64, 128, 192, 256],
            [0, 70, 140, 210, 256])
        self.decr_ch_lut = _create_LUT_8UC1([0, 64, 128, 192, 256],
            [0, 30,  80, 120, 192])
```

The easiest way to make an image appear as if it was taken on a hot, sunny day (maybe close to sunset), is to increase the reds in the image and make the colors appear vivid by increasing the color saturation. We will achieve this in two steps:

1. Increase the pixel values in the R channel and decrease the pixel values in the B channel of an RGB color image using incr_ch_lut and decr_ch_lut, respectively:

    ```
    def render(self, img_rgb):
        c_r, c_g, c_b = cv2.split(img_rgb)
        c_r = cv2.LUT(c_r, self.incr_ch_lut).astype(np.uint8)
        c_b = cv2.LUT(c_b, self.decr_ch_lut).astype(np.uint8)
        img_rgb = cv2.merge((c_r, c_g, c_b))
    ```

2. Transform the image into the **HSV** color space (**H** means hue, **S** means saturation, and **V** means value), and increase the S channel using incr_ch_lut. This can be achieved with the following function, which expects an RGB color image as input:

    ```
    c_b = cv2.LUT(c_b, decrChLUT).astype(np.uint8)

    # increase color saturation
    c_h, c_s, c_v = cv2.split(cv2.cvtColor(img_rgb,
        cv2.COLOR_RGB2HSV))
    c_s = cv2.LUT(c_s, self.incr_ch_lut).astype(np.uint8)
    return cv2.cvtColor(cv2.merge((c_h, c_s, c_v)),
        cv2.COLOR_HSV2RGB)
    ```

The result looks like what is shown here:

Analogously, we can define a cooling filter that increases the pixel values in the B channel, decreases the pixel values in the R channel of an RGB image, converts the image into the HSV color space, and decreases color saturation via the S channel:

```
class CoolingFilter:
    def render(self, img_rgb):
        c_r, c_g, c_b = cv2.split(img_rgb)
        c_r = cv2.LUT(c_r, self.decr_ch_lut).astype(np.uint8)
        c_b = cv2.LUT(c_b, self.incr_ch_lut).astype(np.uint8)
        img_rgb = cv2.merge((c_r, c_g, c_b))
        # decrease color saturation
        c_h, c_s, c_v = cv2.split(cv2.cvtColor(img_rgb,
            cv2.COLOR_RGB2HSV))
        c_s = cv2.LUT(c_s, self.decr_ch_lut).astype(np.uint8)
        return cv2.cvtColor(cv2.merge((c_h, c_s, c_v)),
            cv2.COLOR_HSV2RGB)
```

Now, the result looks like this:

Cartoonizing an image

Over the past few years, professional cartoonizer software has popped up all over the place. In order to achieve the basic cartoon effect, all that we need is a **bilateral filter** and some **edge detection**. The bilateral filter will reduce the color palette, or the numbers of colors that are used in the image. This mimics a cartoon drawing, wherein a cartoonist typically has few colors to work with. Then we can apply edge detection to the resulting image to generate bold silhouettes. The real challenge, however, lies in the computational cost of bilateral filters. We will thus use some tricks to produce an acceptable cartoon effect in real time.

We will adhere to the following procedure to transform an RGB color image into a cartoon:

1. Apply a bilateral filter to reduce the color palette of the image.
2. Convert the original color image into grayscale.
3. Apply a **median blur** to reduce image noise.
4. Use **adaptive thresholding** to detect and emphasize the edges in an edge mask.
5. Combine the color image from step 1 with the edge mask from step 4.

Using a bilateral filter for edge-aware smoothing

A strong bilateral filter is ideally suitable for converting an RGB image into a color painting or a cartoon, because it smoothens flat regions while keeping edges sharp. It seems that the only drawback of this filter is its computational cost, as it is orders of magnitude slower than other smoothing operations, such as a Gaussian blur.

The first measure to take when we need to reduce the computational cost is to perform an operation on an image of low resolution. In order to downscale an RGB image (imgRGB) to a quarter of its size (reduce the width and height to half), we could use cv2.resize:

```
import cv2

img_small = cv2.resize(img_rgb, (0,0), fx=0.5, fy=0.5)
```

A pixel value in the resized image will correspond to the pixel average of a small neighborhood in the original image. However, this process may produce image artifacts, which is also known as aliasing. While this is bad enough on its own, the effect might be enhanced by subsequent processing, for example, edge detection.

A better alternative might be to use the **Gaussian pyramid** for downscaling (again to a quarter of the original size). The Gaussian pyramid consists of a blur operation that is performed before the image is resampled, which reduces aliasing effects:

```
img_small = cv2.pyrDown(img_rgb)
```

However, even at this scale, the bilateral filter might still be too slow to run in real time. Another trick is to repeatedly (say, five times) apply a small bilateral filter to the image instead of applying a large bilateral filter once:

```
num_iter = 5
for _ in xrange(num_iter):
    img_small = cv2.bilateralFilter(img_small, d=9, sigmaColor=9,
        sigmaSpace=7)
```

The three parameters in `cv2.bilateralFilter` control the diameter of the pixel neighborhood (`d`) and the standard deviation of the filter in the color space (`sigmaColor`) and coordinate space (`sigmaSpace`).

Don't forget to restore the image to its original size:

```
img_rgb = cv2.pyrUp(img_small)
```

The result looks like a blurred color painting of a creepy programmer, as follows:

Detecting and emphasizing prominent edges

Again, when it comes to edge detection, the challenge often does not lie in how the underlying algorithm works, but instead which particular algorithm to choose for the task at hand. You might already be familiar with a variety of edge detectors. For example, **Canny edge detection** (`cv2.Canny`) provides a relatively simple and effective method to detect edges in an image, but it is susceptible to noise.

The **Sobel** operator (`cv2.Sobel`) can reduce such artifacts, but it is not rotationally symmetric. The **Scharr** operator (`cv2.Scharr`) was targeted at correcting this, but only looks at the first image derivative. If you are interested, there are even more operators for you, such as the **Laplacian** or **ridge** operator (which includes the second derivative), but they are far more complex. And in the end, for our specific purposes, they might not look better, maybe because they are as susceptible to lighting conditions as any other algorithm.

For the purpose of this project, we will choose a function that might not even be associated with conventional edge detection—`cv2.adaptiveThreshold`. Like `cv2.threshold`, this function uses a threshold pixel value to convert a grayscale image into a binary image. That is, if a pixel value in the original image is above the threshold, then the pixel value in the final image will be 255. Otherwise, it will be 0. However, the beauty of adaptive thresholding is that it does not look at the overall properties of the image. Instead, it detects the most salient features in each small neighborhood independently, without regard to the global image optima. This makes the algorithm extremely robust to lighting conditions, which is exactly what we want when we seek to draw bold, black outlines around objects and people in a cartoon.

However, it also makes the algorithm susceptible to noise. To counteract this, we will preprocess the image with a median filter. A median filter does what its name suggests; it replaces each pixel value with the median value of all the pixels in a small pixel neighborhood. We first convert the RGB image (`img_rgb`) to grayscale (`img_gray`) and then apply a median blur with a seven-pixel local neighborhood:

```
# convert to grayscale and apply median blur
img_gray = cv2.cvtColor(img_rgb, cv2.COLOR_RGB2GRAY)
img_blur = cv2.medianBlur(img_gray, 7)
```

After reducing the noise, it is now safe to detect and enhance the edges using adaptive thresholding. Even if there is some image noise left, the `cv2.ADAPTIVE_THRESH_MEAN_C` algorithm with `blockSize=9` will ensure that the threshold is applied to the mean of a 9 x 9 neighborhood minus `C=2`:

```
img_edge = cv2.adaptiveThreshold(img_blur, 255,
                                 cv2.ADAPTIVE_THRESH_MEAN_C,
                                 cv2.THRESH_BINARY, 9, 2)
```

Downloading the example code

You can download the example code files from your account at http://www.packtpub.com for all the Packt Publishing books you have purchased. If you purchased this book elsewhere, you can visit http://www.packtpub.com/support and register to have the files e-mailed directly to you.

The result of the adaptive thresholding looks like this:

Combining colors and outlines to produce a cartoon

The last step is to combine the two. Simply fuse the two effects together into a single image using cv2.bitwise_and. The complete function is as follows:

```
def render(self, img_rgb):
    numDownSamples = 2 # number of downscaling steps
    numBilateralFilters = 7  # number of bilateral filtering steps

    # -- STEP 1 --
    # downsample image using Gaussian pyramid
    img_color = img_rgb
    for _ in xrange(numDownSamples):
        img_color = cv2.pyrDown(img_color)

    # repeatedly apply small bilateral filter instead of applying
    # one large filter
    for _ in xrange(numBilateralFilters):
        img_color = cv2.bilateralFilter(img_color, 9, 9, 7)

    # upsample image to original size
    for _ in xrange(numDownSamples):
        img_color = cv2.pyrUp(img_color)

    # -- STEPS 2 and 3 --
    # convert to grayscale and apply median blur
    img_gray = cv2.cvtColor(img_rgb, cv2.COLOR_RGB2GRAY)
    img_blur = cv2.medianBlur(img_gray, 7)
```

```
# -- STEP 4 --
# detect and enhance edges
img_edge = cv2.adaptiveThreshold(img_blur, 255,
    cv2.ADAPTIVE_THRESH_MEAN_C, cv2.THRESH_BINARY, 9, 2)

# -- STEP 5 --
# convert back to color so that it can be bit-ANDed
# with color image
img_edge = cv2.cvtColor(img_edge, cv2.COLOR_GRAY2RGB)
return cv2.bitwise_and(img_color, img_edge)
```

The result looks like what is shown here:

Putting it all together

Before we can make use of the designed image filter effects in an interactive way, we need to set up the main script and design a GUI application.

Running the app

To run the application, we will turn to the chapter1.py. script, which we will start by importing all the necessary modules:

```
import numpy as np

import wx
import cv2
```

We will also have to import a generic GUI layout (from `gui`) and all the designed image effects (from `filters`):

```
from gui import BaseLayout
from filters import PencilSketch, WarmingFilter, CoolingFilter,
    Cartoonizer
```

OpenCV provides a straightforward way to access a computer's webcam or camera device. The following code snippet opens the default camera ID (0) of a computer using `cv2.VideoCapture`:

```
def main():
    capture = cv2.VideoCapture(0)
```

On some platforms, the first call to `cv2.VideoCapture` fails to open a channel. In that case, we provide a workaround by opening the channel ourselves:

```
if not(capture.isOpened()):
    capture.open()
```

In order to give our application a fair chance to run in real time, we will limit the size of the video stream to 640 x 480 pixels:

```
capture.set(cv2.cv.CV_CAP_PROP_FRAME_WIDTH, 640)
capture.set(cv2.cv.CV_CAP_PROP_FRAME_HEIGHT, 480)
```

 If you are using OpenCV 3, the constants that you are looking for might be called `cv3.CAP_PROP_FRAME_WIDTH` and `cv3.CAP_PROP_FRAME_HEIGHT`.

Then the `capture` stream can be passed to our GUI application, which is an instance of the `FilterLayout` class:

```
# start graphical user interface
app = wx.App()
layout = FilterLayout(None, -1, 'Fun with Filters', capture)
layout.Show(True)
app.MainLoop()
```

The only thing left to do now is design the said GUI.

The GUI base class

The `FilterLayout` GUI will be based on a generic, plain layout class called `BaseLayout`, which we will be able to use in subsequent chapters as well.

The BaseLayout class is designed as an **abstract base class**. You can think of this class as a blueprint or recipe that will apply to all the layouts that we are yet to design—a skeleton class, if you will, that will serve as the backbone for all of our future GUI code. In order to use abstract classes, we need the following import statement:

```
from abc import ABCMeta, abstractmethod
```

We also include some other modules that will be helpful, especially the wx Python module and OpenCV (of course):

```
import time

import wx
import cv2
```

The class is designed to be derived from the blueprint or skeleton, that is, the wx.Frame class. We also mark the class as abstract by adding the __metaclass__ attribute:

```
class BaseLayout(wx.Frame):
    __metaclass__ = ABCMeta
```

Later on, when we write our own custom layout (FilterLayout), we will use the same notation to specify that the class is based on the BaseLayout blueprint (or skeleton) class, for example, in class FilterLayout(BaseLayout):. But for now, let's focus on the BaseLayout class.

An abstract class has at least one abstract method. An abstract method is akin to specifying that a certain method must exist, but we are not sure at that time what it should look like. For example, suppose BaseLayout contains a method specified as follows:

```
@abstractmethod
def _init_custom_layout(self):
    pass
```

Then any class deriving from it, such as FilterLayout, must specify a fully fleshed-out implementation of a method with that exact signature. This will allow us to create custom layouts, as you will see in a moment.

But first, let's proceed to the GUI constructor.

The GUI constructor

The `BaseLayout` constructor accepts an ID (-1), a title string ('Fun with Filters'), a video capture object, and an optional argument that specifies the number of frames per second. Then, the first thing to do in the constructor is try and read a frame from the captured object in order to determine the image size:

```
def __init__(self, parent, id, title, capture, fps=10):
    self.capture = capture
    # determine window size and init wx.Frame
    _, frame = self.capture.read()
    self.imgHeight,self.imgWidth = frame.shape[:2]
```

We will use the image size to prepare a buffer that will store each video frame as a bitmap, and to set the size of the GUI. Because we want to display a bunch of control buttons below the current video frame, we set the height of the GUI to `self.imgHeight+20`:

```
self.bmp = wx.BitmapFromBuffer(self.imgWidth,
    self.imgHeight, frame)
wx.Frame.__init__(self, parent, id, title,
        size=(self.imgWidth, self.imgHeight+20))
```

We then provide two methods to initialize some more parameters and create the actual layout of the GUI:

```
self._init_base_layout()
self._create_base_layout()
```

Handling video streams

The video stream of the webcam is handled by a series of steps that begin with the `_init_base_layout` method. These steps might appear overly complicated at first, but they are necessary in order to allow the video to run smoothly, even at higher frame rates (that is, to counteract flicker).

The `wxPython` module works with events and callback methods. When a certain event is triggered, it can cause a certain class method to be executed (in other words, a method can *bind* to an event). We will use this mechanism to our advantage and display a new frame every so often using the following steps:

1. We create a timer that will generate a `wx.EVT_TIMER` event whenever 1000./ fps milliseconds have passed:

```
def _init_base_layout(self):
    self.timer = wx.Timer(self)
    self.timer.Start(1000./self.fps)
```

2. Whenever the timer is up, we want the `_on_next_frame` method to be called. It will try to acquire a new video frame:

    ```
    self.Bind(wx.EVT_TIMER, self._on_next_frame)
    ```

3. The `_on_next_frame` method will process the new video frame and store the processed frame in a bitmap. This will trigger another event, `wx.EVT_PAINT`. We want to bind this event to the `_on_paint` method, which will paint the display the new frame:

    ```
    self.Bind(wx.EVT_PAINT, self._on_paint)
    ```

The `_on_next_frame` method grabs a new frame and, once done, sends the frame to another method, `_process_frame`, for further processing:

```
def _on_next_frame(self, event):
    ret, frame = self.capture.read()
    if ret:
        frame = self._process_frame(cv2.cvtColor(frame,
            cv2.COLOR_BGR2RGB))
```

The processed frame (`frame`) is then stored in a bitmap buffer (`self.bmp`):

```
self.bmp.CopyFromBuffer(frame)
```

Calling `Refresh` triggers the aforementioned `wx.EVT_PAINT` event, which binds to `_on_paint`:

```
self.Refresh(eraseBackground=False)
```

The paint method then grabs the frame from the buffer and displays it:

```
def _on_paint(self, event):
    deviceContext = wx.BufferedPaintDC(self.pnl)
    deviceContext.DrawBitmap(self.bmp, 0, 0)
```

A basic GUI layout

The creation of the generic layout is done by a method called `_create_base_layout`. The most basic layout consists of only a large black panel that provides enough room to display the video feed:

```
def _create_base_layout(self):
    self.pnl = wx.Panel(self, -1,
                        size=(self.imgWidth, self.imgHeight))
    self.pnl.SetBackgroundColour(wx.BLACK)
```

In order for the layout to be extendable, we add it to a vertically arranged `wx.BoxSizer` object:

```
self.panels_vertical = wx.BoxSizer(wx.VERTICAL)
self.panels_vertical.Add(self.pnl, 1, flag=wx.EXPAND)
```

Next, we specify an abstract method, `_create_custom_layout`, for which we will not fill in any code. Instead, any user of our base class can make their own custom modifications to the basic layout:

```
self._create_custom_layout()
```

Then, we just need to set the minimum size of the resulting layout and center it:

```
self.SetMinSize((self.imgWidth, self.imgHeight))
self.SetSizer(self.panels_vertical)
self.Centre()
```

A custom filter layout

Now we are almost done! If we want to use the `BaseLayout` class, we need to provide code for the three methods that were left blank previously:

- `_init_custom_layout`: This is where we can initialize task-specific parameters
- `_create_custom_layout`: This is where we can make task-specific modifications to the GUI layout
- `_process_frame`: This is where we perform task-specific processing on each captured frame of the camera feed

At this point, initializing the image filters is self-explanatory, as it only requires us to instantiate the corresponding classes:

```
def _init_custom_layout(self):
    self.pencil_sketch = PencilSketch((self.imgWidth,
        self.imgHeight))
    self.warm_filter = WarmingFilter()
    self.cool_filter = CoolingFilter()
    self.cartoonizer = Cartoonizer()
```

To customize the layout, we arrange a number of radio buttons horizontally, one button per image effect mode:

```
def _create_custom_layout(self):
    # create a horizontal layout with all filter modes
    pnl = wx.Panel(self, -1 )
```

```
self.mode_warm = wx.RadioButton(pnl, -1, 'Warming Filter',
    (10, 10), style=wx.RB_GROUP)
self.mode_cool = wx.RadioButton(pnl, -1, 'Cooling Filter',
    (10, 10))
self.mode_sketch = wx.RadioButton(pnl, -1, 'Pencil Sketch',
    (10, 10))
self.mode_cartoon = wx.RadioButton(pnl, -1, 'Cartoon',
    (10, 10))
hbox = wx.BoxSizer(wx.HORIZONTAL)
hbox.Add(self.mode_warm, 1)
hbox.Add(self.mode_cool, 1)
hbox.Add(self.mode_sketch, 1)
hbox.Add(self.mode_cartoon, 1)
pnl.SetSizer(hbox)
```

Here, the `style=wx.RB_GROUP` option makes sure that only one of these radio buttons can be selected at a time.

To make these changes take effect, `pnl` needs to be added to list of existing panels:

```
self.panels_vertical.Add(pnl, flag=wx.EXPAND | wx.BOTTOM | wx.TOP,
        border=1)
```

The last method to be specified is `_process_frame`. Recall that this method is triggered whenever a new camera frame is received. All that we need to do is pick the right image effect to be applied, which depends on the radio button configuration. We simply check which of the buttons is currently selected and call the corresponding render method:

```
def _process_frame(self, frame_rgb):
    if self.mode_warm.GetValue():
        frame = self.warm_filter.render(frame_rgb)
    elif self.mode_cool.GetValue():
        frame = self.cool_filter.render(frame_rgb)
    elif self.mode_sketch.GetValue():
        frame = self.pencil_sketch.render(frame_rgb)
    elif self.mode_cartoon.GetValue():
        frame = self.cartoonizer.render(frame_rgb)
```

Don't forget to return the processed frame:

```
return frame
```

And we're done!

Here is the result:

Summary

In this chapter, we explored a number of interesting image processing effects. We used dodging and burning to create a black-and-white pencil sketch effect, explored lookup tables to arrive at an efficient implementation of curve filters, and got creative to produce a cartoon effect.

In the next chapter, we will shift gears a bit and explore the use of depth sensors, such as Microsoft Kinect 3D, to recognize hand gestures in real time.

2

Hand Gesture Recognition Using a Kinect Depth Sensor

The goal of this chapter is to develop an app that detects and tracks simple hand gestures in real time using the output of a depth sensor, such as that of a Microsoft Kinect 3D sensor or an Asus Xtion. The app will analyze each captured frame to perform the following tasks:

- **Hand region segmentation**: The user's hand region will be extracted in each frame by analyzing the **depth map** output of the Kinect sensor, which is done by **thresholding**, applying some **morphological operations**, and finding **connected components**

- **Hand shape analysis**: The shape of the segmented hand region will be analyzed by determining **contours**, **convex hull**, and **convexity defects**

- **Hand gesture recognition**: The number of extended fingers will be determined based on the hand contour's **convexity defects**, and the gesture will be classified accordingly (with no extended fingers corresponding to a fist, and five extended fingers corresponding to an open hand)

Gesture recognition is an ever-popular topic in computer science. This is because it not only enables humans to communicate with machines (human-machine interaction or HMI), but also constitutes the first step for machines to begin understanding human body language. With affordable sensors such as Microsoft Kinect or Asus Xtion, and open source software such as OpenKinect and OpenNI, it has never been easy to get started in the field yourself. So, what shall we do with all this technology?

The beauty of the algorithm that we are going to implement in this chapter is that it works well for a number of hand gestures, yet is simple enough to run in real time on a generic laptop. Also, if we want, we can easily extend it to incorporate more complicated hand pose estimations. The end product looks like this:

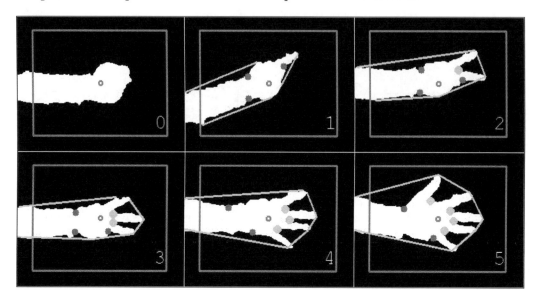

No matter how many fingers of my left hand I extend, the algorithm correctly segments the hand region (white), draws the corresponding convex hull (the green line surrounding the hand), finds all convexity defects that belong to the spaces between fingers (large green points) while ignoring others (small red points), and infers the correct number of extended fingers (the number in the bottom-right corner), even for a fist.

This chapter assumes that you have a Microsoft Kinect 3D sensor installed. Alternatively, you may install an Asus Xtion or any other depth sensor for which OpenCV has built-in support. First, install OpenKinect and libfreenect from http://www.openkinect.org/wiki/Getting_Started. Then, you need to build (or rebuild) OpenCV with OpenNI support. The GUI used in this chapter will again be designed with wxPython, which can be obtained from http://www.wxpython.org/download.php.

Planning the app

The final app will consist of the following modules and scripts:

- `gestures`: A module that consists of an algorithm for recognizing hand gestures. We separate this algorithm from the rest of the application so that it can be used as a standalone module without the need for a GUI.

- `gestures.HandGestureRecognition`: A class that implements the entire process flow of hand-gesture recognition. It accepts a single-channel depth image (acquired from the Kinect depth sensor) and returns an annotated RGB color image with an estimated number of extended fingers.

- `gui`: A module that provides a wxPython GUI application to access the capture device and display the video feed. This is the same module that we used in the last chapter. In order to have it access the Kinect depth sensor instead of a generic camera, we will have to extend some of the base class functionality.

- `gui.BaseLayout`: A generic layout from which more complicated layouts can be built.

- `chapter2`: The main script for the chapter.

- `chapter2.KinectLayout`: A custom layout based on `gui.BaseLayout` that displays the Kinect depth sensor feed. Each captured frame is processed with the `HandGestureRecognition` class described earlier.

- `chapter2.main`: The main function routine for starting the GUI application and accessing the depth sensor.

Setting up the app

Before we can get down to the nitty-gritty of our gesture recognition algorithm, we need to make sure that we can access the Kinect sensor and display a stream of depth frames in a simple GUI.

Accessing the Kinect 3D sensor

Accessing Microsoft Kinect from within OpenCV is not much different from accessing a computer's webcam or camera device. The easiest way to integrate a Kinect sensor with OpenCV is by using an `OpenKinect` module called `freenect`. For installation instructions, take a look at the preceding information box. The following code snippet grants access to the sensor using `cv2.VideoCapture`:

```
import cv2
import freenect


device = cv2.cv.CV_CAP_OPENNI
capture = cv2.VideoCapture(device)
```

On some platforms, the first call to `cv2.VideoCapture` fails to open a capture channel. In this case, we provide a workaround by opening the channel ourselves:

```
if not(capture.isOpened(device)):
    capture.open(device)
```

If you want to connect to your Asus Xtion, the `device` variable should be assigned the `cv2.cv.CV_CAP_OPENNI_ASUS` value instead.

In order to give our app a fair chance of running in real time, we will limit the frame size to 640 x 480 pixels:

```
capture.set(cv2.cv.CV_CAP_PROP_FRAME_WIDTH, 640)
capture.set(cv2.cv.CV_CAP_PROP_FRAME_HEIGHT, 480)
```

 If you are using OpenCV 3, the constants you are looking for might be called `cv3.CAP_PROP_FRAME_WIDTH` and `cv3.CAP_PROP_FRAME_HEIGHT`.

The `read()` method of `cv2.VideoCapture` is inappropriate when we need to synchronize a set of cameras or a multihead camera, such as a Kinect. In this case, we should use the `grab()` and `retrieve()` methods instead. An even easier approach when working with `OpenKinect` is to use the `sync_get_depth()` and `sync_get_video()` methods.

For the purpose of this chapter, we will need only the Kinect's depth map, which is a single-channel (grayscale) image in which each pixel value is the estimated distance from the camera to a particular surface in the visual scene. The latest frame can be grabbed via this code:

```
depth, timestamp = freenect.sync_get_depth()
```

The preceding code returns both the depth map and a timestamp. We will ignore the latter for now. By default, the map is in 11-bit format, which is inadequate to be visualized with `cv2.imshow` right away. Thus, it is a good idea to convert the image to 8-bit precision first.

In order to reduce the range of depth values in the frame, we will clip the maximal distance to a value of 1,023 (or `2**10-1`). This will get rid of values that correspond either to noise or distances that are far too large to be of interest to us:

```
np.clip(depth, 0, 2**10-1, depth)
depth >>= 2
```

Then, we will convert the image into 8-bit format and display it:

```
depth = depth.astype(np.uint8)
cv2.imshow("depth", depth)
```

Running the app

In order to run our app, we will need to execute a main function routine that accesses the Kinect, generates the GUI, and executes the main loop of the app. This is done by the main function of `chapter2.py`:

```
import numpy as np

import wx
import cv2
import freenect

from gui import BaseLayout
from gestures import HandGestureRecognition


def main():
    device = cv2.cv.CV_CAP_OPENNI
    capture = cv2.VideoCapture()
    if not(capture.isOpened()):
        capture.open(device)

    capture.set(cv2.cv.CV_CAP_PROP_FRAME_WIDTH, 640)
    capture.set(cv2.cv.CV_CAP_PROP_FRAME_HEIGHT, 480)
```

As in the last chapter, we will design a suitable layout (KinectLayout) for the current project:

```
# start graphical user interface
app = wx.App()
layout = KinectLayout(None, -1, 'Kinect Hand Gesture
    Recognition', capture)
layout.Show(True)
app.MainLoop()
```

The Kinect GUI

The layout chosen for the current project (KinectLayout) is as plain as it gets. It should simply display the live stream of the Kinect depth sensor at a comfortable frame rate of 10 frames per second. Therefore, there is no need to further customize BaseLayout:

```
class KinectLayout(BaseLayout):
    def _create_custom_layout(self):
        pass
```

The only parameter that needs to be initialized this time is the recognition class. This will be useful in just a moment:

```
def _init_custom_layout(self):
    self.hand_gestures = HandGestureRecognition()
```

Instead of reading a regular camera frame, we need to acquire a depth frame via the freenect method sync_get_depth(). This can be achieved by overriding the following method:

```
def _acquire_frame(self):
```

As mentioned earlier, by default this function returns a single-channel depth image with 11-bit precision and a timestamp. However, we are not interested in the timestamp, and we simply pass on the frame if the acquisition is successful:

```
frame, _ = freenect.sync_get_depth()
# return success if frame size is valid
if frame is not None:
    return (True, frame)
else:
    return (False, frame)
```

The rest of the visualization pipeline is handled by the `BaseLayout` class. We only need to make sure that we provide a `_process_frame` method. This method accepts a depth image with 11-bit precision, processes it, and returns an annotated 8-bit RGB color image. Conversion to a regular grayscale image is the same as mentioned in the previous subsection:

```
def _process_frame(self, frame):
    # clip max depth to 1023, convert to 8-bit grayscale
    np.clip(frame, 0, 2**10 - 1, frame)
    frame >>= 2
    frame = frame.astype(np.uint8)
```

The resulting grayscale image can then be passed to the hand gesture recognizer, which will return the estimated number of extended fingers (`num_fingers`) and the annotated RGB color image mentioned earlier (`img_draw`):

```
num_fingers, img_draw = self.hand_gestures.recognize(frame)
```

In order to simplify the segmentation task of the `HandGestureRecognition` class, we will instruct the user to place their hand in the center of the screen. To provide a visual aid for this, let's draw a rectangle around the image center and highlight the center pixel of the image in orange:

```
height, width = frame.shape[:2]
cv2.circle(img_draw, (width/2, height/2), 3, [255, 102, 0], 2)
cv2.rectangle(img_draw, (width/3, height/3), (width*2/3,
        height*2/3), [255, 102, 0], 2)
```

In addition, we will print `num_fingers` on the screen:

```
cv2.putText(img_draw, str(num_fingers), (30, 30),
        cv2.FONT_HERSHEY_SIMPLEX, 1, (255, 255, 255))

return img_draw
```

Tracking hand gestures in real time

Hand gestures are analyzed by the `HandGestureRecognition` class, especially by its `recognize` method. This class starts off with a few parameter initializations, which will be explained and used later:

```
class HandGestureRecognition:
    def __init__(self):
        # maximum depth deviation for a pixel to be considered
            # within range
```

```
self.abs_depth_dev = 14

# cut-off angle (deg): everything below this is a
    convexity
# point that belongs to two extended fingers
self.thresh_deg = 80.0
```

The `recognize` method is where the real magic takes place. This method handles the entire process flow, from the raw grayscale image all the way to a recognized hand gesture. It implements the following procedure:

1. It extracts the user's hand region by analyzing the depth map (`img_gray`) and returning a hand region mask (`segment`):

    ```
    def recognize(self, img_gray):
        segment = self._segment_arm(img_gray)
    ```

2. It performs contour analysis on the hand region mask (`segment`). Then, it returns the largest contour area found in the image (`contours`) and any convexity defects (`defects`):

    ```
    [contours, defects] = self._find_hull_defects(segment)
    ```

3. Based on the contours found and the convexity defects, it detects the number of extended fingers (`num_fingers`) in the image. Then, it annotates the output image (`img_draw`) with contours, defect points, and the number of extended fingers:

    ```
    img_draw = cv2.cvtColor(img_gray, cv2.COLOR_GRAY2RGB)
    [num_fingers, img_draw] =
        self._detect_num_fingers(contours,
            defects, img_draw)
    ```

4. It returns the estimated number of extended fingers (`num_fingers`), as well as the annotated output image (`img_draw`):

    ```
    return (num_fingers, img_draw)
    ```

Hand region segmentation

The automatic detection of an arm, and later the hand region, could be designed to be arbitrarily complicated, maybe by combining information about the shape and color of an arm or hand. However, using a skin color as a determining feature to find hands in visual scenes might fail terribly in poor lighting conditions or when the user is wearing gloves. Instead, we choose to recognize the user's hand by its shape in the depth map. Allowing hands of all sorts to be present in any region of the image unnecessarily complicates the mission of the present chapter, so we make two simplifying assumptions:

- We will instruct the user of our app to place their hand in front of the center of the screen, orienting their palm roughly parallel to the orientation of the Kinect sensor so that it is easier to identify the corresponding depth layer of the hand.

- We will also instruct the user to sit roughly one to two meters away from the Kinect, and to slightly extend their arm in front of their body so that the hand will end up in a slightly different depth layer than the arm. However, the algorithm will still work even if the full arm is visible.

In this way, it will be relatively straightforward to segment the image based on the depth layer alone. Otherwise, we would have to come up with a hand detection algorithm first, which would unnecessarily complicate our mission. If you feel adventurous, feel free to do this on your own.

Finding the most prominent depth of the image center region

Once the hand is placed roughly in the center of the screen, we can start finding all image pixels that lie on the same depth plane as the hand.

To do this, we simply need to determine the most prominent depth value of the center region of the image. The simplest approach would be as follows: look only at the depth value of the center pixel:

```
width, height = depth.shape
center_pixel_depth = depth[width/2, height/2]
```

Then, create a mask in which all pixels at a depth of `center_pixel_depth` are white and all others are black:

```
import numpy as np

depth_mask = np.where(depth == center_pixel_depth, 255,
    0).astype(np.uint8)
```

However, this approach will not be very robust, because chances are that it will be compromised by the following:

- Your hand will not be placed perfectly parallel to the Kinect sensor
- Your hand will not be perfectly flat
- The Kinect sensor values will be noisy

Therefore, different regions of your hand will have slightly different depth values.

The `_segment_arm` method takes a slightly better approach; that is, looking at a small neighborhood in the center of the image and determining the median (meaning the most prominent) depth value. First, we find the center region (for example, 21 x 21 pixels) of the image frame:

```
def _segment_arm(self, frame):
    """ segments the arm region based on depth """
    center_half = 10 # half-width of 21 is 21/2-1
    lowerHeight = self.height/2 - center_half
    upperHeight = self.height/2 + center_half
    lowerWidth = self.width/2 - center_half
    upperWidth = self.width/2 + center_half
    center = frame[lowerHeight:upperHeight,
        lowerWidth:upperWidth]
```

We can then reshape the depth values of this center region into a one-dimensional vector and determine the median depth value, `med_val`:

```
med_val = np.median(center)
```

We can now compare `med_val` with the depth value of all pixels in the image and create a mask in which all pixels whose depth values are within a particular range `[med_val-self.abs_depth_dev, med_val+self.abs_depth_dev]` are white, and all other pixels are black. However, for reasons that will be come clear in a moment, let's paint the pixels gray instead of white:

```
frame = np.where(abs(frame - med_val) <= self.abs_depth_dev,
    128, 0).astype(np.uint8)
```

The result will look like this:

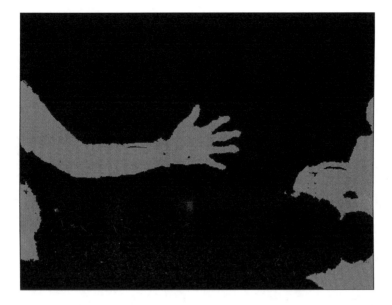

Applying morphological closing to smoothen the segmentation mask

A common problem with segmentation is that a hard threshold typically results in small imperfections (that is, holes, as in the preceding image) in the segmented region. These holes can be alleviated by using morphological opening and closing. Opening removes small objects from the foreground (assuming that the objects are bright on a dark foreground), whereas closing removes small holes (dark regions).

This means that we can get rid of the small black regions in our mask by applying morphological closing (dilation followed by erosion) with a small 3 x 3 pixel kernel:

```
kernel = np.ones((3, 3), np.uint8)
frame = cv2.morphologyEx(frame, cv2.MORPH_CLOSE, kernel)
```

The result looks a lot smoother, as follows:

Notice, however, that the mask still contains regions that do not belong to the hand or arm, such as what appears to be one of my knees on the left and some furniture on the right. These objects just happen to be on the same depth layer as my arm and hand. If possible, we could now combine the depth information with another descriptor, maybe a texture-based or skeleton-based hand classifier, that would weed out all non-skin regions.

Finding connected components in a segmentation mask

An easier approach is to realize that most of the time hands are not connected to knees or furniture. We already know that the center region belongs to the hand, so we can simply apply `cv2.floodfill` to find all the connected image regions.

Before we do this, we want to be absolutely certain that the seed point for the flood fill belongs to the right mask region. This can be achieved by assigning a grayscale value of 128 to the seed point. However, we also want to make sure that the center pixel does not, by any coincidence, lie within a cavity that the morphological operation failed to close. So, let's set a small 7 x 7 pixel region with a grayscale value of 128 instead:

```
small_kernel = 3
frame[self.height/2-small_kernel :
          self.height/2+small_kernel,
          self.width/2-small_kernel :
          self.width/2+small_kernel] = 128
```

As flood filling (as well as morphological operations) is potentially dangerous, later OpenCV versions require the specification of a mask that avoids *flooding* the entire image. This mask has to be 2 pixels wider and taller than the original image and has to be used in combination with the cv2.FLOODFILL_MASK_ONLY flag. It can be very helpful in constraining the flood filling to a small region of the image or a specific contour so that we need not connect two neighboring regions that should have never been connected in the first place. It's better to be safe than sorry, right?

Ah, screw it! Today, we feel courageous! Let's make the mask entirely black:

```
mask = np.zeros((self.height+2, self.width+2), np.uint8)
```

Then, we can apply the flood fill to the center pixel (the seed point) and paint all the connected regions white:

```
flood = frame.copy()
cv2.floodFill(flood, mask, (self.width/2, self.height/2),
    255, flags=4 | (255 << 8))
```

At this point, it should be clear why we decided to start with a gray mask earlier. We now have a mask that contains white regions (arm and hand), gray regions (neither arm nor hand but other things in the same depth plane), and black regions (all others). With this setup, it is easy to apply a simple binary threshold to highlight only the relevant regions of the pre-segmented depth plane:

```
ret, flooded = cv2.threshold(flood, 129, 255, cv2.THRESH_BINARY)
```

This is what the resulting mask looks like:

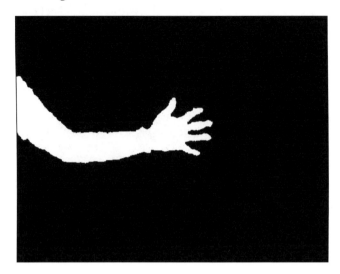

The resulting segmentation mask can now be returned to the `recognize` method, where it will be used as an input to `_find_hull_defects`, as well as a canvas for drawing the final output image (`img_draw`).

Hand shape analysis

Now that we know (roughly) where the hand is located, we aim to learn something about its shape.

Determining the contour of the segmented hand region

The first step involves determining the contour of the segmented hand region. Luckily, OpenCV comes with a pre-canned version of such an algorithm — `cv2.findContours`. This function acts on a binary image and returns a set of points that are believed to be part of the contour. As there might be multiple contours present in the image, it is possible to retrieve an entire hierarchy of contours:

```
def _find_hull_defects(self, segment):
    contours, hierarchy = cv2.findContours(segment,
        cv2.RETR_TREE, cv2.CHAIN_APPROX_SIMPLE)
```

Furthermore, because we do not know which contour we are looking for, we have to make an assumption to clean up the contour result. Since it is possible that some small cavities are left over even after the morphological closing—but we are fairly certain that our mask contains only the segmented area of interest—we will assume that the largest contour found is the one that we are looking for. Thus, we simply traverse the list of contours, calculate the contour area (cv2.contourArea), and store only the largest one (max_contour):

```
max_contour = max(contours, key=cv2.contourArea)
```

Finding the convex hull of a contour area

Once we have identified the largest contour in our mask, it is straightforward to compute the convex hull of the contour area. The convex hull is basically the envelope of the contour area. If you think of all the pixels that belong to the contour area as a set of nails sticking out of a board, then the convex hull is the shape formed by a tight rubber band that surrounds all the nails.

We can get the convex hull directly from our largest contour (max_contour):

```
hull = cv2.convexHull(max_contour, returnPoints=False)
```

As we now want to look at convexity deficits in this hull, we are instructed by the OpenCV documentation to set the returnPoints optional flag to False.

The convex hull drawn in yellow around a segmented hand region looks like this:

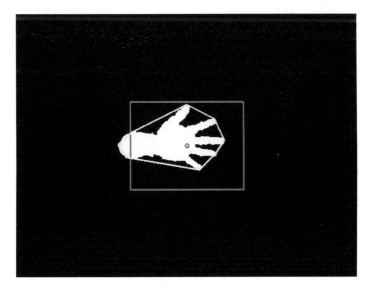

Finding the convexity defects of a convex hull

As is evident from the preceding screenshot, not all points on the convex hull belong to the segmented hand region. In fact, all the fingers and the wrist cause severe *convexity defects*, that is, points of the contour that are far away from the hull.

We can find these defects by looking at both the largest contour (`max_contour`) and the corresponding convex hull (`hull`):

```
defects = cv2.convexityDefects(max_contour, hull)
```

The output of this function (`defects`) is a 4-tuple that contains `start_index` (the point of the contour where the defect begins), `end_index` (the point of the contour where the defect ends), `farthest_pt_index` (the farthest from the convex hull point within the defect), and `fixpt_depth` (the distance between the farthest point and the convex hull). We will make use of this information in just a moment when we try to extract the number of extended fingers.

For now though, our job is done. The extracted contour (`max_contour`) and convexity defects (`defects`) can be passed to `recognize`, where they will be used as inputs to `_detect_num_fingers`:

```
return (cnt,defects)
```

Hand gesture recognition

What remains to be done is to classify the hand gesture based on the number of extended fingers. For example, if we find five extended fingers, we assume the hand to be open, whereas no extended fingers implies a fist. All that we are trying to do is count from zero to five and make the app recognize the corresponding number of fingers.

This is actually trickier than it might seem at first. For example, people in Europe might count to three by extending their thumb, index finger, and middle finger. If you do that in the US, people there might get horrendously confused, because they do not tend to use their thumbs when signaling the number two. This might lead to frustration, especially in restaurants (trust me). If we could find a way to generalize these two scenarios—maybe by appropriately counting the number of extended fingers—we would have an algorithm that could teach simple hand gesture recognition to not only a machine but also (maybe) to an average waitress.

As you might have guessed, the answer is related to convexity defects. As mentioned earlier, extended fingers cause defects in the convex hull. However, the inverse is not true; that is, not all convexity defects are caused by fingers! There might be additional defects caused by the wrist, as well as the overall orientation of the hand or the arm. How can we distinguish between these different causes of defects?

Distinguishing between different causes of convexity defects

The trick is to look at the angle between the farthest point from the convex hull point within the defect (farthest_pt_index) and the start and end points of the defect (start_index and end_index, respectively), as illustrated in the following screenshot:

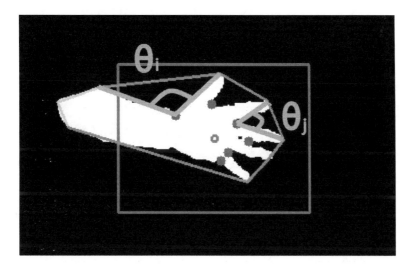

In this screenshot, the orange markers serve as a visual aid to center the hand in the middle of the screen, and the convex hull is outlined in green. Each red dot corresponds to *the point farthest from the convex hull* (farthest_pt_index) for every convexity defect detected. If we compare a typical angle that belongs to two extended fingers (such as **θj**) to an angle that is caused by general hand geometry (such as **θi**), we notice that the former is much smaller than the latter. This is obviously because humans can spread their fingers only a little, thus creating a narrow angle made by the farthest defect point and the neighboring fingertips.

Therefore, we can iterate over all convexity defects and compute the angle between the said points. For this, we will need a utility function that calculates the angle (in radians) between two arbitrary, list-like vectors, v1 and v2:

```
def angle_rad(v1, v2):
    return np.arctan2(np.linalg.norm(np.cross(v1, v2)),
        np.dot(v1, v2))
```

This method uses the cross product to compute the angle, rather than doing it in the standard way. The standard way of calculating the angle between two vectors v1 and v2 is by calculating their dot product and dividing it by the norm of v1 and the norm of v2. However, this method has two imperfections:

- You have to manually avoid division by zero if either the norm of v1 or the norm of v2 is zero

- The method returns relatively inaccurate results for small angles

Similarly, we provide a simple function to convert an angle from degrees to radians:

```
def deg2rad(angle_deg):
    return angle_deg/180.0*np.pi
```

Classifying hand gestures based on the number of extended fingers

What remains to be done is actually to classify the hand gesture based on the number of extended fingers. The _detect_num_fingers method will take as input the detected contour (contours), the convexity defects (defects), and a canvas to draw on (img_draw):

```
def _detect_num_fingers(self, contours, defects, img_draw):
```

Based on these parameters, it will then determine the number of extended fingers.

However, we first need to define a cut-off angle that can be used as a threshold to classify convexity defects as being caused by extended fingers or not. Except for the angle between the thumb and the index finger, it is rather hard to get anything close to 90 degrees, so anything close to that number should work. We do not want the cut-off angle to be too high, because that might lead to misclassifications:

```
self.thresh_deg = 80.0
```

For simplicity, let's focus on the special cases first. If we do not find any convexity defects, it means that we possibly made a mistake during the convex hull calculation, or there are simply no extended fingers in the frame, so we return 0 as the number of detected fingers:

```
if defects is None:
    return [0, img_draw]
```

However, we can take this idea even further. Due to the fact that arms are usually slimmer than hands or fists, we can assume that the hand geometry will always generate at least two convexity defects (which usually belong to the wrists). So, if there are no additional defects, it implies that there are no extended fingers:

```
if len(defects) <= 2:
    return [0, img_draw]
```

Now that we have ruled out all special cases, we can begin counting real fingers. If there is a sufficient number of defects, we will find a defect between every pair of fingers. Thus, in order to get the number right (num_fingers), we should start counting at 1:

```
num_fingers = 1
```

Then, we can start iterating over all convexity defects. For each defect, we will extract the four elements and draw its hull for visualization purposes:

```
for i in range(defects.shape[0]):
    # each defect point is a 4-tuplestart_idx, end_idx,
        farthest_idx, _ == defects[i, 0]
    start = tuple(contours[start_idx][0])
    end = tuple(contours[end_idx][0])
    far = tuple(contours[farthest_idx][0])

    # draw the hull
    cv2.line(img_draw, start, end [0, 255, 0], 2)
```

Then, we will compute the angle between the two edges from far to start and from far to end. If the angle is smaller than self.thresh_deg degrees, it means that we are dealing with a defect that is most likely caused by two extended fingers. In such cases, we want to increment the number of detected fingers (num_fingers), and draw the point with green. Otherwise, we draw the point with red:

```
# if angle is below a threshold, defect point belongs
# to two extended fingers
if angle_rad(np.subtract(start, far),
        np.subtract(end, far))
        < deg2rad(self.thresh_deg):
    # increment number of fingers
```

```
    num_fingers = num_fingers + 1

    # draw point as green
    cv2.circle(img_draw, far, 5, [0, 255, 0], -1)
else:
    # draw point as red
    cv2.circle(img_draw, far, 5, [255, 0, 0], -1)
```

After iterating over all convexity defects, we pass the number of detected fingers and the assembled output image to the `recognize` method:

```
return (min(5, num_fingers), img_draw)
```

This will make sure that we do not exceed the common number of fingers per hand.

The result can be seen in the following screenshots:

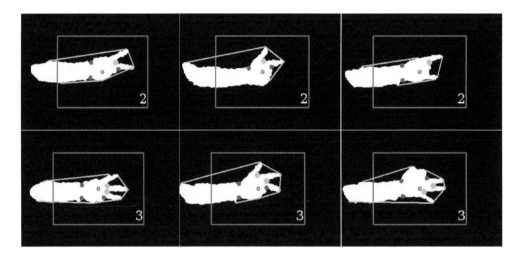

Interestingly, our app is able to detect the correct number of extended fingers in a variety of hand configurations. Defect points between extended fingers are easily classified as such by the algorithm, and others are successfully ignored.

Summary

This chapter showed a relatively simple and yet surprisingly robust way of recognizing a variety of hand gestures by counting the number of extended fingers.

The algorithm first shows how a task-relevant region of the image can be segmented using depth information acquired from a Microsoft Kinect 3D Sensor, and how morphological operations can be used to clean up the segmentation result. By analyzing the shape of the segmented hand region, the algorithm comes up with a way to classify hand gestures based on the types of convexity effects found in the image. Once again, mastering our use of OpenCV to perform a desired task did not require us to produce a large amount of code. Instead, we were challenged to gain an important insight that made us use the built-in functionality of OpenCV in the most effective way possible.

Gesture recognition is a popular but challenging field in computer science, with applications in a large number of areas, such as human-computer interaction, video surveillance, and even the video game industry. You can now use your advanced understanding of segmentation and structure analysis to build your own state-of-the-art gesture recognition system.

In the next chapter, we will continue to focus on detecting objects of interest in visual scenes, but we will assume a much more complicated case—viewing the object from an arbitrary perspective and distance. To do this, we will combine perspective transformations with scale-invariant feature descriptors to develop a robust feature-matching algorithm.

3
Finding Objects via Feature Matching and Perspective Transforms

The goal of this chapter is to develop an app that is able to detect and track an object of interest in the video stream of a webcam, even if the object is viewed from different angles or distances or under partial occlusion.

In this chapter, we will cover the following topics:

- Feature extraction
- Feature matching
- Feature tracking

In the previous chapter, you learned how to detect and track a simple object (the silhouette of a hand) in a very controlled environment. To be more specific, we instructed the user of our app to place the hand in the central region of the screen and made assumptions about the size and shape of the object (the hand). But what if we wanted to detect and track objects of arbitrary sizes, possibly viewed from a number of different angles or under partial occlusion?

For this, we will make use of feature descriptors, which are a way of capturing the important properties of our object of interest. We do this so that the object can be located even when it is embedded in a busy visual scene. We will again apply our algorithm to the live stream of a webcam, and do our best to keep the algorithm robust yet simple enough to run in real time.

Tasks performed by the app

The app will analyze each captured frame to perform the following tasks:

- **Feature extraction**: We will describe an object of interest with **Speeded-Up Robust Features** (**SURF**), which is an algorithm used to find distinctive **keypoints** in an image that are both scale invariant and rotation invariant. These keypoints will help us make sure that we are tracking the right object over multiple frames. Because the appearance of the object might change from time to time, it is important to find keypoints that do not depend on the viewing distance or viewing angle of the object (hence the scale and rotation invariance).

- **Feature matching**: We will try to establish a correspondence between keypoints using the **Fast Library for Approximate Nearest Neighbors** (**FLANN**) to see whether a frame contains keypoints similar to the keypoints from our object of interest. If we find a good match, we will mark the object in each frame.

- **Feature tracking**: We will keep track of the located object of interest from frame to frame using various forms of **early outlier detection** and **outlier rejection** to speed up the algorithm.

- **Perspective transform**: We will then reverse any translations and rotations that the object has undergone by **warping the perspective** so that the object appears upright in the center of the screen. This creates a cool effect in which the object seems frozen in a position while the entire surrounding scene rotates around it.

An example of the first three steps is shown in the following image, which contains a template image of our object of interest on the left, and me holding a printout of the template image on the right. Matching features in the two frames are connected with blue lines, and the located object is outlined in green on the right:

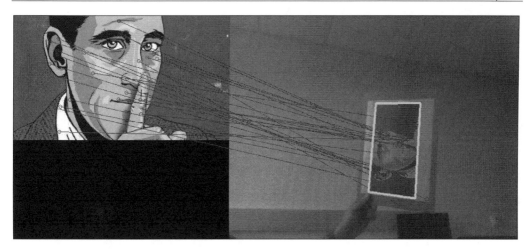

The last step is transforming the located object so that it is projected onto the frontal plane (which should look roughly like the original template image, appearing close-up and roughly upright), while the entire scene seems to warp around it, as shown in the following figure:

> Again, the GUI will be designed with wxPython 2.8, which can be obtained from http://www.wxpython.org/ download.php. This chapter has been tested with OpenCV 2.4.9. Note that if you are using OpenCV 3, you may have to obtain the so-called *extra* modules from https://github.com/Itseez/opencv_contrib and install OpenCV 3 with the OPENCV_EXTRA_MODULES_PATH variable set in order to get SURF and FLANN installed. Also, note that you may have to obtain a license to use SURF in commercial applications.

Planning the app

The final app will consist of a Python class for detecting, matching, and tracking image features, as well as a wxPython GUI application that accesses the webcam and displays each processed frame.

The project will contain the following modules and scripts:

- feature_matching: A module containing an algorithm for feature extraction, feature matching, and feature tracking. We separate this algorithm from the rest of the application so that it can be used as a standalone module without the need for a GUI.

- feature_matching.FeatureMatching: A class that implements the entire feature-matching process flow. It accepts an RGB camera frame and tries to locate an object of interest in it.

- gui: A module that provides a wxPython GUI application to access the capture device and display the video feed. This is the same module that we used in previous chapters.

- gui.BaseLayout: A generic layout from which more complicated layouts can be built. This chapter does not require any modifications to the basic layout.

- chapter3: The main script for the chapter.

- chapter3.FeatureMatchingLayout: A custom layout based on gui. BaseLayout that displays the webcam video feed. Each captured frame will be processed with the FeatureMatching class described earlier.

- chapter3.main: The main function routine for starting the GUI application and accessing the depth sensor.

Setting up the app

Before we can get down to the nitty-gritty of our feature-matching algorithm, we need to make sure that we can access the webcam and display the video stream in a simple GUI. Luckily, we have already figured out how to do this in *Chapter 1*, *Fun with Filters*.

Running the app

In order to run our app, we will need to execute a main function routine that accesses the webcam, generates the GUI, and executes the main loop of the app:

```
import cv2
import wx

from gui import BaseLayout
from feature_matching import FeatureMatching


def main():
    capture = cv2.VideoCapture(0)
    if not(capture.isOpened()):
        capture.open()

    capture.set(cv2.cv.CV_CAP_PROP_FRAME_WIDTH, 640)
    capture.set(cv2.cv.CV_CAP_PROP_FRAME_HEIGHT, 480)

    # start graphical user interface
    app = wx.App()

    layout = FeatureMatchingLayout(None, -1, 'Feature Matching',
        capture)
    layout.Show(True)
    app.MainLoop()
```

 If you are using OpenCV 3, the constants that you are looking for might be called `cv3.CAP_PROP_FRAME_WIDTH` and `cv3.CAP_PROP_FRAME_HEIGHT`.

The FeatureMatching GUI

Analogous to the previous chapter, the layout chosen for the current project (FeatureMatchingLayout) is as plain as it gets. It should simply display the video feed of the webcam at a comfortable frame rate of 10 frames per second. Therefore, there is no need to further customize BaseLayout:

```
class FeatureMatchingLayout(BaseLayout):
    def _create_custom_layout(self):
        pass
```

The only parameter that needs to be initialized this time is the feature-matching class. We pass to it the path to a template (or training) file that depicts the object of interest:

```
def _init_custom_layout(self):
    self.matching = FeatureMatching
        (train_image='salinger.jpg')
```

The rest of the visualization pipeline is handled by the BaseLayout class. We only need to make sure that we provide a _process_frame method. This method accepts a RGB color image, processes it by means of the FeatureMatching method match, and passes the processed image for visualization. If the object is detected in the current frame, the match method will report success=True and we will return the processed frame. If the match method is not successful, we will simply return the input frame:

```
def _process_frame(self, frame):
    self.matching = FeatureMatching
        (train_image='salinger.jpg')
    # if object detected, display new frame, else old one
    success, new_frame = self.matching.match(frame)
    if success:
        return new_frame
    else:
        return frame
```

The process flow

Features are extracted, matched, and tracked by the `FeatureMatching` class, especially by its public `match` method. However, before we can begin analyzing the incoming video stream, we have some homework to do. It might not be clear right away what some of these things mean (especially for SURF and FLANN), but we will discuss these steps in detail in the following sections. For now, we only have to worry about initialization:

```
class FeatureMatching:
    def __init__(self, train_image='salinger.jpg'):
```

1. This sets up a SURF detector (see the next section for details) with a Hessian threshold between 300 and 500:

   ```
   self.min_hessian = 400
   self.SURF = cv2.SURF(self.min_hessian)
   ```

2. We load a template of our object of interest (`self.img_obj`), or print an error if it cannot be found:

   ```
   self.img_obj = cv2.imread(train_image, cv2.CV_8UC1)
   if self.img_obj is None:
       print "Could not find train image " + train_image
           raise SystemExit
   ```

3. Also, store the shape of the image (`self.sh_train`) for convenience:

   ```
   self.sh_train = self.img_train.shape[:2]   # rows, cols
   ```

   For reasons that will soon be evidently clear, we will call the template image the **train image** and every incoming frame a **query image**. The train image has a size of 480 x 270 pixels and looks like this:

4. Apply SURF to the object of interest. This can be done with a convenient function call that returns both a list of keypoints and the descriptor (see the next section for details):

```
self.key_train, self.desc_train =
    self.SURF.detectAndCompute(self.img_obj, None)
```

We will do the same with each incoming frame and compare lists of features across images.

5. Set up a FLANN object (see the next section for details). This requires the specification of some additional parameters via dictionaries, such as which algorithm to use and how many trees to run in parallel:

```
FLANN_INDEX_KDTREE = 0
index_params = dict(algorithm = FLANN_INDEX_KDTREE,
    trees = 5)
search_params = dict(checks=50)
self.flann = cv2.FlannBasedMatcher(index_params,
    search_params)
```

6. Finally, initialize some additional bookkeeping variables. These will come in handy when we want to make our feature tracking both quicker and more accurate. For example, we will keep track of the latest computed homography matrix and of the number of frames we have spent without locating our object of interest (see the next section for details):

```
self.last_hinv = np.zeros((3,3))
self.num_frames_no_success = 0
self.max_frames_no_success = 5
self.max_error_hinv = 50.
```

Then, the bulk of the work is done by the `FeatureMatching` method `match`. This method follows the procedure elaborated here:

1. It extracts interesting image features from each incoming video frame. This is done in `FeatureMatching._extract_features`.

2. It matches features between the template image and the video frame. This is done in `FeatureMatching._match_features`. If no such match is found, it skips to the next frame.

3. It finds the corner points of the template image in the video frame. This is done in `FeatureMatching._detect_corner_points`. If any of the corners lies (significantly) outside the frame, it skips to the next frame.

4. It calculates the area of the quadrilateral that the four corner points span. If the area is either too small or too large, it skips to the next frame.

5. It outlines the corner points of the template image in the current frame.

6. It finds the perspective transform that is necessary to bring the located object from the current frame to the `frontoparallel` plane. This is done in `FeatureMatching._warp_keypoints`. If the result is significantly different from the result we got recently for an earlier frame, it skips to the next frame.

7. It warps the perspective of the current frame to make the object of interest appear centered and upright.

In the following sections, we will discuss these steps in detail.

Feature extraction

Generally speaking, a feature is an *interesting area* of an image. It is a measurable property of an image that is very informative about what the image represents. Usually, the grayscale value of an individual pixel (the *raw data*) does not tell us a lot about the image as a whole. Instead, we need to derive a property that is more informative.

For example, knowing that there are patches in the image that look like eyes, a nose, and a mouth will allow us to reason about how likely it is that the image represents a face. In this case, the number of resources required to describe the data (are we seeing an image of a face?) is drastically reduced (does the image contain two eyes? a nose? a mouth?).

More low-level features, such as the presence of edges, corners, blobs, or ridges, may be more informative generally. Some features may be better than others, depending on the application. Once we have made up our mind on how to describe our favorite feature, we need to come up with a way to check whether or not the image contains such features and where it contains them.

Feature detection

The process of finding areas of interest in an image is called feature detection. OpenCV provides a whole range of feature detection algorithms, such as these:

- **Harris corner detection**: Knowing that edges are areas with high-intensity changes in all directions, Harris and Stephens came up with a fast way of finding such areas. This algorithm is implemented as `cv2.cornerHarris` in OpenCV.

- **Shi-Tomasi corner detection**: Shi and Tomasi have their own idea of what are good features to track, and they usually do better than Harris corner detection by finding the N strongest corners. This algorithm is implemented as `cv2.goodFeaturesToTrack` in OpenCV.

- **Scale-Invariant Feature Transform (SIFT)**: Corner detection is not sufficient when the scale of the image changes. To this end, Lowe developed a method to describe keypoints in an image that are independent of orientation and size (hence the name **scale invariant**).The algorithm is implemented as cv2.SIFT in OpenCV2, but was moved to the *extra* modules in OpenCV3 since its code is proprietary.

- **Speeded-Up Robust Features (SURF)**: SIFT has proven to be really good, but it is not fast enough for most applications. This is where SURF comes in, which replaces the expensive Laplacian of a Gaussian from SIFT with a box filter. The algorithm is implemented as cv2.SURF in OpenCV2, but, like SIFT, it was moved to the *extra* modules in OpenCV3 since its code is proprietary.

OpenCV has support for even more feature descriptors, such as **Features from Accelerated Segment Test (FAST)**, **Binary Robust Independent Elementary Features (BRIEF)**, and **Oriented FAST and Rotated BRIEF (ORB)**, the latter being an open source alternative to SIFT or SURF.

Detecting features in an image with SURF

In the remainder of this chapter, we will make use of the SURF detector.

The SURF algorithm can be roughly divided into two distinctive steps: detecting points of interest, and formulating a descriptor. SURF relies on the Hessian corner detector for interest point detection, which requires the setting of a min_hessian threshold. This threshold determines how large the output from the Hessian filter must be in order for a point to be used as an interest point. A larger value results in fewer but (theoretically) more salient interest points, whereas a smaller value results in more numerous but less salient points. Feel free to experiment with different values. In this chapter, we will choose a value of 400, as seen earlier in FeatureMatching.__init__, where we created a SURF descriptor with the following code snippet:

```
self.min_hessian = 400
self.SURF = cv2.SURF(self.min_hessian)
```

Both the features and the descriptor can then be obtained in a single step, for example, on an input image img_query without the use of a mask (None):

```
key_query, desc_query = self.SURF.detectAndCompute
    (img_query, None)
```

In OpenCV 2.4.8 or later, we can now easily draw the keypoints with the following function:

```
imgOut = cv2.drawKeypoints(img_query, key_query, None,
    (255, 0, 0), 4)
cv2.imshow(imgOut)
```

> Make sure that you check `len(keyQuery)` first, as SURF might return a large number of features. If you care only about drawing the keypoints, try setting `min_hessian` to a large value until the number of returned keypoints is manageable.
>
> If our OpenCV distribution is older than that, we might have to write our own function. Note that SURF is protected by patent laws. Therefore, if you wish to use SURF in a commercial application, you will be required to obtain a license.

Feature matching

Once we have extracted features and their descriptors from two (or more) images, we can start asking whether some of these features show up in both (or all) images. For example, if we have descriptors for both our object of interest (`self.desc_train`) and the current video frame (`desc_query`), we can try to find regions of the current frame that look like our object of interest. This is done by the following method, which makes use of the **Fast Library for Approximate Nearest Neighbors (FLANN)**:

```
good_matches = self._match_features(desc_query)
```

The process of finding frame-to-frame correspondences can be formulated as the search for the nearest neighbor from one set of descriptors for every element of another set.

The first set of descriptors is usually called the train set, because in machine learning, these descriptors are used to train some model, such as the model of the object that we want to detect. In our case, the train set corresponds to the descriptor of the template image (our object of interest). Hence, we call our template image the *train image* (`self.img_train`).

The second set is usually called the query set, because we continually ask whether it contains our train image. In our case, the query set corresponds to the descriptor of each incoming frame. Hence, we call a frame the *query image* (`img_query`).

Features can be matched in any number of ways, for example, with the help of a brute-force matcher (`cv2.BFMatcher`) that looks for each descriptor in the first set and the closest descriptor in the second set by trying each one (exhaustive search).

Matching features across images with FLANN

The alternative is to use an approximate **k-nearest neighbor** (kNN) algorithm to find correspondences, which is based on the fast third-party library FLANN. A FLANN match is performed with the following code snippet, where we use kNN with `k=2`:

```
def _match_features(self, desc_frame):
    matches = self.flann.knnMatch(self.desc_train, desc_frame,
        k=2)
```

The result of `flann.knnMatch` is a list of correspondences between two sets of descriptors, both contained in the `matches` variable. These are the train set, because it corresponds to the pattern image of our object of interest, and the query set, because it corresponds to the image in which we are searching for our object of interest.

The ratio test for outlier removal

The more the correct matches found (which means that more pattern-to-image correspondences exist), the more the chances that the pattern is present in the image. However, some matches might be false positives.

A well-known technique for removing outliers is called the ratio test. Since we performed kNN-matching with k=2, the two nearest descriptors are returned for each match. The first match is the closest neighbor and the second match is the second closest neighbor. Intuitively, a correct match will have a much closer first neighbor than its second closest neighbor. On the other hand, the two closest neighbors will be at a similar distance from an incorrect match. Therefore, we can find out how good a match is by looking at the difference between the distances. The **ratio test** says that the match is good only if the distance ratio between the first match and the second match is smaller than a given number (usually around 0.5); in our case, this number chosen to be 0.7. To remove all matches that do not satisfy this requirement, we filter the list of matches and store the good matches in the `good_matches` variable:

```
# discard bad matches, ratio test as per Lowe's paper
good_matches = filter(lambda x: x[0].distance<0.7*x[1].distance,
    matches)
```

Then we pass the matches we found to `FeatureMatching.match` so that they can be processed further:

```
return good_matches
```

Visualizing feature matches

In newer versions of OpenCV, we can easily draw matches using `cv2.drawMatches` or `cv3.drawMatchesKnn`.

In older versions of OpenCV, we may need to write our own function. The goal is to draw both the object of interest and the current video frame (in which we expect the object to be embedded) next to each other:

```python
def draw_good_matches(img1, kp1, img2, kp2, matches):
    # Create a new output image that concatenates the
    # two images together (a.k.a) a montage
    rows1, cols1 = img1.shape[:2]
    rows2, cols2 = img2.shape[:2]
    out = np.zeros((max([rows1, rows2]), cols1+cols2, 3),
        dtype='uint8')
```

In order to draw colored lines on the image, we create a three-channel RGB image:

```python
    # Place the first image to the left, copy 3x for RGB
    out[:rows1, :cols1, :] = np.dstack([img1, img1, img1])

    # Place the next image to the right of it, copy 3x for RGB
    out[:rows2, cols1:cols1 + cols2, :] = np.dstack([img2, img2,
        img2])
```

Then, for each pair of points between both images, we draw small blue circles, and we connect the two circles with a line. For this, we have to iterate over the list of matching keypoints. The keypoints are stored as tuples in Python, with two entries for the x and y coordinates. Each match, `m`, stores the index in the keypoint lists, where `m.trainIdx` points to the index in the first keypoint list (`kp1`) and `m.queryIdx` points to the index in the second keypoint list (`kp2`):

```python
for m in matches:
    # Get the matching keypoints for each of the images
    c1, r1 = kp1[m.trainIdx].pt
    c2, r2 = kp2[m.queryIdx].pt
```

With the correct indices, we can now draw a circle at the correct location (with the radius as 4, the color as blue, and the thickness as 1) and connect the circles with a line:

```python
    radius = 4
    BLUE = (255, 0, 0)
    thickness = 1
    # Draw a small circle at both co-ordinates
    cv2.circle(out, (int(c1), int(r1)), radius, BLUE, thickness)
```

```
cv2.circle(out, (int(c2) + cols1, int(r2)), radius, BLUE,
    thickness

# Draw a line in between the two points
cv2.line(out, (int(c1), int(r1)), (int(c2) + cols1, int(r2)),
    BLUE, thickness)
return out
```

Then, the returned image can be drawn with this code:

```
cv2.imshow('imgFlann', draw_good_matches(self.img_train,
    self.key_train, img_query, key_query, good_matches))
```

The blue lines connect the features in the object (left) to the features in the scenery (right), as shown here:

This works fine in a simple example such as this, but what happens when there are other objects in the scene? Since our object contains some lettering that seems highly salient, what happens when there are other words present?

As it turns out, the algorithm works even under such conditions, as you can see in this screenshot:

Interestingly, the algorithm did not confuse the name of the author as seen on the left with the black-on-white lettering next to the book in the scene, even though they spell out the same name. This is because the algorithm found a description of the object that does not rely purely on the grayscale representation. On the other hand, an algorithm doing a pixel-wise comparison could have easily gotten confused.

Homography estimation

Since we are assuming that the object of our interest is planar (an image) and rigid, we can find the homography transformation between the feature points of the two images. Homography will calculate the perspective transformation required to bring all feature points in the object image (`self.key_train`) into the same plane as all the feature points in the current image frame (`self.key_query`). But first, we need to find the image coordinates of all keypoints that are good matches:

```
def _detect_corner_points(self, key_frame, good_matches):
    src_points = [self.key_train[good_matches[i].trainIdx].pt
        for i in xrange(len(good_matches))]
```

```
dst_points = [keyQuery[good_matches[i].queryIdx].pt
    for i in xrange(len(good_matches))]
```

To find the correct perspective transformation (a homography matrix H), the cv2.findHomography function will use the **random sample consensus** (**RANSAC**) method to probe different subsets of input points:

```
H, _ = cv2.findHomography(np.array(src_points),
    np.array(dst_points), cv2.RANSAC)
```

The homography matrix H can then help us transform any point in the pattern into the scenery, such as transforming a corner point in the training image to a corner point in the query image. In other words, this means that we can draw the outline of the book cover in the query image by transforming the corner points from the training image! For this, we take the list of corner points of the training image (src_corners) and see where they are projected in the query image by performing a perspective transform:

```
self.sh_train = self.img_train.shape[:2]  # rows, cols
src_corners = np.array([(0,0), (self.sh_train[1],0),
    (self.sh_train[1],self.sh_train[0]), (0,self.sh_train[0])],
    dtype=np.float32)
dst_corners = cv2.perspectiveTransform(src_corners[None, :, :],
    H)
```

The dst_corners return argument is a list of image points. All that we need to do is draw a line between each point in dst_corners and the very next one, and we will have an outline in the scenery. But first, in order to draw the line at the right image coordinates, we need to offset the *x* coordinate by the width of the pattern image (because we are showing the two images next to each other):

```
dst_corners = map(tuple,dst_corners[0])
dst_corners = [(np.int(dst_corners[i][0]+self.sh_train[1]),
    np.int(dst_corners[i][1]))
```

Then we can draw the lines from the *ith* point to the *(i+1)-th* point in the list (wrapping around to 0):

```
for i in xrange(0,len(dst_corners)):
    cv2.line(img_flann, dst_corners[i], dst_corners[(i+1) % 4],
        (0, 255, 0), 3)
```

Finally, we draw the outline of the book cover, like this:

This works even when the object is only partially visible, as follows:

Warping the image

We can also do the opposite—going from the probed scenery to the training pattern coordinates. This makes it possible for the book cover to be brought onto the frontal plane, as if we were looking at it directly from above. To achieve this, we can simply take the inverse of the homography matrix to get the inverse transformation:

```
Hinv = cv2.linalg.inverse(H)
```

However, this would map the top-left corner of the book cover to the origin of our new image, which would cut off everything to the left of and above the book cover. Instead, we want to roughly center the book cover in the image. Thus, we need to calculate a new homography matrix. As input, we will have our `pts_scene` scenery points. As output, we want an image that has the same shape as the pattern image:

```
dst_size = img_in.shape[:2]   # cols, rows
```

The book cover should be roughly half of that size. We can come up with a scaling factor and a bias term so that every keypoint in the scenery image is mapped to the correct coordinate in the new image:

```
scale_row = 1./src_size[0]*dst_size[0]/2.
bias_row = dst_size[0]/4.
scale_col = 1./src_size[1]*dst_size[1]/2.
bias_col = dst_size[1]/4.
```

Next, we just need to apply this linear scaling to every keypoint in the list. The easiest way to do this is with list comprehensions:

```
src_points = [key_frame[good_matches[i].trainIdx].pt
    for i in xrange(len(good_matches))]
dst_points = [self.key_train[good_matches[i].queryIdx].pt
    for i in xrange(len(good_matches))]
dst_points = [[x*scale_row+bias_row, y*scale_col+bias_col]
    for x, y in dst_points]
```

Then we can find the homography matrix between these points (make sure that the list is converted to a NumPy array):

```
Hinv, _ = cv2.findHomography(np.array(src_points),
    np.array(dst_points), cv2.RANSAC)
```

After that, we can use the homography matrix to transform every pixel in the image (this is also called warping the image):

```
img_warp = cv2.warpPerspective(img_query, Hinv, dst_size)
```

The result looks like this (matching on the left and warped image on the right):

The image resulting from the perspective transformation might not be perfectly aligned with the `frontoparallel` plane, because after all, the homography matrix is only approximate. In most cases, however, our approach works just fine, such as in the example shown in the following figure:

Feature tracking

Now that our algorithm works for single frames, how can we make sure that the image found in one frame will also be found in the very next frame?

In `FeatureMatching.__init__`, we created some bookkeeping variables that we said we would use for feature tracking. The main idea is to enforce some coherence while going from one frame to the next. Since we are capturing roughly 10 frames per second, it is reasonable to assume that the changes from one frame to the next will not be too radical. Therefore, we can be sure that the result we get in any given frame has to be similar to the result we got in the previous frame. Otherwise, we discard the result and move on to the next frame.

However, we have to be careful not to get stuck with a result that we think is reasonable but is actually an outlier. To solve this problem, we keep track of the number of frames we have spent without finding a suitable result. We use `self.num_frames_no_success`; if this number is smaller than a certain threshold, say `self.max_frames_no_success`, we do the comparison between the frames. If it is greater than the threshold, we assume that too much time has passed since the last result was obtained, in which case it would be unreasonable to compare the results between the frames.

Early outlier detection and rejection

We can extend the idea of outlier rejection to every step in the computation. The goal then becomes minimizing the workload while maximizing the likelihood that the result we obtain is a good one.

The resulting procedure for early outlier detection and rejection is embedded in `FeatureMatching.match` and looks as follows:

```
def match(self, frame):
    # create a working copy (grayscale) of the frame
    # and store its shape for convenience
    img_query = cv2.cvtColor(frame, cv2.COLOR_BGR2GRAY)
    sh_query = img_query.shape[:2]  # rows,cols
```

1. Find good matches between the feature descriptors of the pattern and the query image:

   ```
   key_query, desc_query = self._extract_features(img_query)
   good_matches = self._match_features(descQuery)
   ```

   In order for RANSAC to work in the very next step, we need at least four matches. If fewer matches are found, we admit defeat and return `False` right away:

   ```
   if len(good_matches) < 4:
       self.num_frames_no_success=
           self.num_frames_no_success + 1
       return False, frame
   ```

2. Find the corner points of the pattern in the query image (`dst_corners`):

```
dst_corners = self._detect_corner_points(key_query,
    good_matches)
```

If any of these points lies significantly outside the image (by 20 pixels in our case), it means that either we are not looking at our object of interest, or the object of interest is not entirely in the image. In both cases, we have no interest in proceeding, and we return `False`:

```
if np.any(filter(lambda x: x[0] < -20 or x[1] < -20
    or x[0] > sh_query[1] + 20 or x[1] > sh_query[0] + 20,
    dst_corners)):
        self.num_frames_no_success =
            self.num_frames_no_success + 1
        return False, frame
```

3. If the four recovered corner points do not span a reasonable quadrilateral (a polygon with four sides), it means that we are probably not looking at our object of interest. The area of a quadrilateral can be calculated with this code:

```
area = 0
for i in xrange(0, 4):
    next_i = (i + 1) % 4
    area = area + (dst_corners[i][0]*dst_corners[next_i][1]
        - dst_corners[i][1]*dst_corners[next_i][0])/2.
```

If the area is either unreasonably small or unreasonably large, we discard the frame and return `False`:

```
if area < np.prod(sh_query)/16. or area >
    np.prod(sh_query)/2.:
        self.num_frames_no_success=
            self.num_frames_no_success + 1
        return False, frame
```

4. If the recovered homography matrix is too different from the one that we last recovered (`self.last_hinv`), it means that we are probably looking at a different object, in which case we discard the frame and return `False`. We compare the current homography matrix to the last one by calculating the distance between the two matrices:

```
np.linalg.norm(Hinv - self.last_hinv)
```

However, we only want to consider `self.last_hinv` if it is fairly recent, say, from within the last `self.max_frames_no_success`. This is why we keep track of `self.num_frames_no_success`:

```
recent = self.num_frames_no_success <
    self.max_frames_no_success
```

```
        similar = np.linalg.norm(Hinv - self.last_hinv) <
            self.max_error_hinv
    if recent and not similar:
        self.num_frames_no_success =
            self.num_frames_no_success + 1
        return False, frame
```

This will help us keep track of the one and the same object of interest over time. If, for any reason, we lose track of the pattern image for more than `self.max_frames_no_success` frames, we skip this condition and accept whatever homography matrix was recovered up to that point. This makes sure that we do not get stuck with some `self.last_hinv` matrix that is actually an outlier.

Otherwise, we can be fairly certain that we have successfully located the object of interest in the current frame. In such a case, we store the homography matrix and reset the counter:

```
    self.num_frames_no_success = 0
    self.last_hinv = Hinv
```

All that is left to do is warping the image and (for the first time) returning `True` along with the warped image so that the image can be plotted:

```
    img_out = cv2.warpPerspective(img_query, Hinv, dst_size)
    img_out = cv2.cvtColor(img_out, cv2.COLOR_GRAY2RGB)
    return True, imgOut
```

Seeing the algorithm in action

The result of the matching procedure in a live stream from my laptop's webcam looks like this:

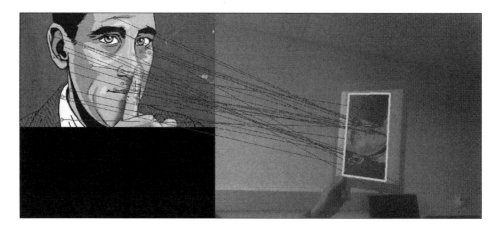

As you can see, most of the keypoints in the pattern image were matched correctly with their counterparts in the query image on the right. The printout of the pattern can now be slowly moved around, tilted, and turned. As long as all the corner points stay in the current frame, the homography matrix is updated accordingly and the outline of the pattern image is drawn correctly.

This works even if the printout is upside down, as shown here:

In all cases, the warped image brings the pattern image to an upright, centered position on the frontoparallel plane. This creates a cool effect of having the pattern image frozen in place in the center of the screen, while the surroundings twist and turn around it, like this:

In most cases, the warped image looks fairly accurate, as seen in the one earlier. If, for any reason, the algorithm accepts a wrong homography matrix that leads to an unreasonably warped image, then the algorithm will discard the outlier and recover within half a second (that is, within `self.max_frames_no_success` frames), leading to accurate and efficient tracking throughout.

Summary

This chapter showed a robust feature tracking method that is fast enough to run in real time when applied to the live stream of a webcam.

First, the algorithm shows you how to extract and detect important features in an image independently of perspective and size, be it in a template of our object of interest (train image) or a more complex scene in which we expect the object of interest to be embedded (query image). A match between feature points in the two images is then found by clustering the keypoints using a fast version of the nearest neighbor algorithm. From there on, it is possible to calculate a perspective transformation that maps one set of feature points to the other. With this information, we can outline the train image as found in the query image and warp the query image so that the object of interest appears upright in the center of the screen.

With this in hand, we now have a good starting point for designing a cutting-edge feature tracking, image stitching, or augmented-reality application.

In the next chapter, we will continue studying the geometrical features of a scene, but this time, we will be concentrating on motion. Specifically, we will study how to reconstruct a scene in 3D by inferring its geometrical features from camera motion. For this, we will have to combine our knowledge of feature matching with optic flow and structure-from-motion techniques.

4

3D Scene Reconstruction Using Structure from Motion

The goal of this chapter is to study how to reconstruct a scene in 3D by inferring the geometrical features of the scene from camera motion. This technique is sometimes referred to as **structure from motion**. By looking at the same scene from different angles, we will be able to infer the real-world 3D coordinates of different features in the scene. This process is known as **triangulation**, which allows us to **reconstruct** the scene as a **3D point cloud**.

In the previous chapter, you learned how to detect and track an object of interest in the video stream of a webcam, even if the object is viewed from different angles or distances, or under partial occlusion. Here, we will take the tracking of interesting features a step further and consider what we can learn about the entire visual scene by studying similarities between image frames. If we take two pictures of the same scene from different angles, we can use **feature matching** or **optic flow** to estimate any translational and rotational movement that the camera underwent between taking the two pictures. However, in order for this to work, we will first have to calibrate our camera.

The complete procedure involves the following steps:

1. **Camera calibration**: We will use a chessboard pattern to extract the intrinsic camera matrix as well as the distortion coefficients, which are important for performing the scene reconstruction.

2. **Feature matching**: We will match points in two 2D images of the same visual scene, either via **Speeded-Up Robust Features (SURF)** or via optic flow, as seen in the following image:

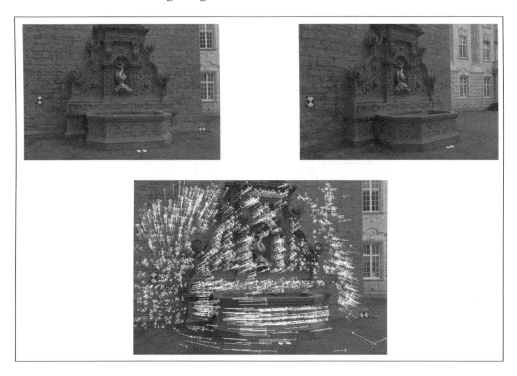

3. **Image rectification**: By estimating the camera motion from a pair of images, we will extract the **essential matrix** and rectify the images.

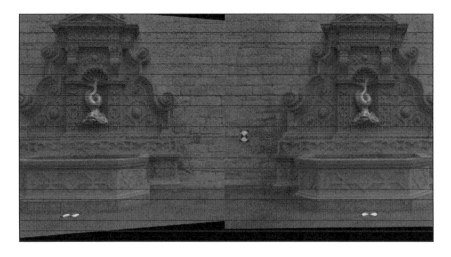

4. **Triangulation**: We will reconstruct the 3D real-world coordinates of the image points by making use of constraints from **epipolar geometry**.

5. **3D point cloud visualization**: Finally, we will visualize the recovered 3D structure of the scene using scatterplots in matplotlib, which is most compelling when studied using pyplot's **Pan axes** button. This button lets you rotate and scale the point cloud in all three dimensions. It is a little harder to visualize in still frames, as can be seen in the following figure (left panel: standing slightly in front to the left side of the fountain, center panel: looking down on the fountain, right panel: standing slightly in front to the right of the fountain):

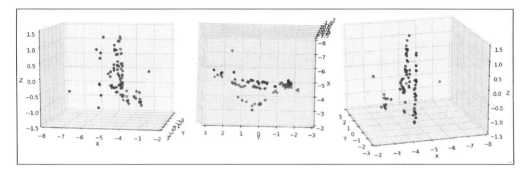

 This chapter has been tested with OpenCV 2.4.9 and wxPython 2.8 (`http://www.wxpython.org/download.php`). It also requires NumPy (`http://www.numpy.org`) and matplotlib (`http://www.matplotlib.org/downloads.html`). Note that if you are using OpenCV3, you may have to obtain the so-called *extra* modules from `https://github.com/Itseez/opencv_contrib` and install OpenCV3 with the `OPENCV_EXTRA_MODULES_PATH` variable set in order to get SURF installed. Also note that you may have to obtain a license to use SURF in commercial applications.

Planning the app

The final app will extract and visualize structure from motion on a pair of images. We will assume that these two images have been taken with the same camera, whose internal camera parameters we know. If these parameters are not known, they need to be estimated first in a camera calibration process.

The final app will then consist of the following modules and scripts:

- `chapter4.main`: This is the main function routine for starting the application.

- `scene3D.SceneReconstruction3D`: This is a class that contains a range of functionalities for calculating and visualizing structure from motion. It includes the following public methods:
  - `__init__`: This constructor will accept the intrinsic camera matrix and the distortion coefficients
  - `load_image_pair`: A method used to load from the file, two images that have been taken with the camera described earlier
  - `plot_optic_flow`: A method used to visualize the optic flow between the two image frames
  - `draw_epipolar_lines`: A method used to draw the epipolar lines of the two images
  - `plot_rectified_images`: A method used to plot a rectified version of the two images

- `plot_point_cloud`: This is a method used to visualize the recovered real-world coordinates of the scene as a 3D point cloud. In order to arrive at a 3D point cloud, we will need to exploit epipolar geometry. However, epipolar geometry assumes the pinhole camera model, which no real camera follows. We need to rectify our images to make them look as if they have come from a pinhole camera. For that, we need to estimate the parameters of the camera, which leads us to the field of camera calibration.

Camera calibration

So far, we have worked with whatever image came straight out of our webcam, without questioning the way in which it was taken. However, every camera lens has unique parameters, such as focal length, principal point, and lens distortion. What happens behind the covers when a camera takes a picture, is that; light falls through a lens, followed by an aperture, before falling on the surface of a light sensor. This process can be approximated with the pinhole camera model. The process of estimating the parameters of a real-world lens such that it would fit the pinhole camera model is called camera calibration (or **camera resectioning**, and it should not be confused with photometric camera calibration).

The pinhole camera model

The **pinhole camera model** is a simplification of a real camera in which there is no lens and the camera aperture is approximated by a single point (the pinhole). When viewing a real-world 3D scene (such as a tree), light rays pass through the point-sized aperture and fall on a 2D image plane inside the camera, as seen in the following diagram:

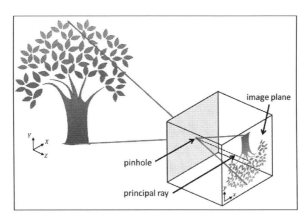

In this model, a 3D point with coordinates (X,Y,Z) is mapped to a 2D point with coordinates (x,y) that lies on the **image plane**. Note that this leads to the tree appearing upside down on the image plane. The line that is perpendicular to the image plane, and passes through the pinhole is called the **principal ray**, and its length is called the **focal length**. The focal length is a part of the internal camera parameters, as it may vary depending on the camera being used.

Hartley and Zisserman found a mathematical formula to describe how a 2D point with coordinates (x,y) can be inferred from a 3D point with coordinates (X,Y,Z) and the camera's intrinsic parameters, as follows:

$$\begin{bmatrix} x \\ y \\ w \end{bmatrix} = \begin{bmatrix} f_x & 0 & c_x \\ 0 & f_y & c_y \\ 0 & 0 & 1 \end{bmatrix} \begin{bmatrix} X \\ Y \\ Z \end{bmatrix}$$

For now, let's focus on the 3 x 3 matrix in the preceding formula, which is the **intrinsic camera matrix**—a matrix that compactly describes all internal camera parameters. The matrix comprises focal lengths (`fx` and `fy`) and optical centers (`cx` and `cy`) expressed in pixel coordinates. As mentioned earlier, the focal length is the distance between the pinhole and the image plane. A true pinhole camera has only one focal length, in which case `fx = fy = f`. However, in reality, these two values might differ, maybe due to flaws in the digital camera sensor. The point at which the principal ray intersects the image plane is called the principal point, and its relative position on the image plane is captured by the optical center (or principal point offset).

In addition, a camera might be subject to radial or tangential distortion, leading to a *fish-eye* effect. This is because of hardware imperfections and lens misalignments. These distortions can be described with a list of the **distortion coefficients**. Sometimes, radial distortions are actually a desired artistic effect. At other times, they need to be corrected.

 For more information on the pinhole camera model, there are many good tutorials out there on the Web, such as `http://ksimek.github.io/2013/08/13/intrinsic`.

Because these parameters are specific to the camera hardware (hence the name intrinsic), we need to calculate them only once in the lifetime of a camera. This is called **camera calibration**.

Estimating the intrinsic camera parameters

In OpenCV, camera calibration is fairly straightforward. The official documentation provides a good overview of the topic and some sample C++ scripts at `http://docs.opencv.org/doc/tutorials/calib3d/camera_calibration/camera_calibration.html`.

For educational purposes, we will develop our own calibration script in Python. We will need to present a special pattern image, with a known geometry (chessboard plate or black circles on a white background), to the camera we wish to calibrate. Because we know the geometry of the pattern image, we can use feature detection to study the properties of the internal camera matrix. For example, if the camera suffers from undesired radial distortion, the different corners of the chessboard pattern will appear distorted in the image and not lie on a rectangular grid. By taking about 10 to 20 snapshots of the chessboard pattern from different points of view, we can collect enough information to correctly infer the camera matrix and the distortion coefficients.

For this, we will use the `calibrate.py` script. Analogous to previous chapters, we will use a simple layout (`CameraCalibration`) based on `BaseLayout` that embeds a webcam video stream. The main function of the script will generate the GUI and execute the main loop of the app:

```
import cv2
import numpy as np
import wx

from gui import BaseLayout


def main():
    capture = cv2.VideoCapture(0)
    if not(capture.isOpened()):
        capture.open()

    capture.set(cv2.cv.CV_CAP_PROP_FRAME_WIDTH, 640)
    capture.set(cv2.cv.CV_CAP_PROP_FRAME_HEIGHT, 480)

    # start graphical user interface
    app = wx.App()
    layout = CameraCalibration(None, -1, 'Camera Calibration',
        capture)
    layout.Show(True)
    app.MainLoop()
```

 If you are using OpenCV 3, the constants that you are looking for might be called `cv3.CAP_PROP_FRAME_WIDTH` and `cv3.CAP_PROP_FRAME_HEIGHT`.

The camera calibration GUI

The GUI is a customized version of the generic `BaseLayout`:

```
class CameraCalibration(BaseLayout):
```

The layout consists of only the current camera frame and a single button below it. This button allows us to start the calibration process:

```
def _create_custom_layout(self):
    """Creates a horizontal layout with a single button"""
    pnl = wx.Panel(self, -1)
    self.button_calibrate = wx.Button(pnl,
        label='Calibrate Camera')
```

```
self.Bind(wx.EVT_BUTTON, self._on_button_calibrate)
hbox = wx.BoxSizer(wx.HORIZONTAL)
hbox.Add(self.button_calibrate)
pnl.SetSizer(hbox)
```

For these changes to take effect, `pnl` needs to be added to the list of existing panels:

```
self.panels_vertical.Add(pnl, flag=wx.EXPAND | wx.BOTTOM |
    wx.TOP, border=1)
```

The rest of the visualization pipeline is handled by the `BaseLayout` class. We only need to make sure that we provide the `_init_custom_layout` and `_process_frame` methods.

Initializing the algorithm

In order to perform the calibration process, we need to do some bookkeeping. For now, let's focus on a single 10 x 7 chessboard. The algorithm will detect all the 9 x 6 inner corners of the chessboard (referred to as *object points*) and store the detected image points of these corners in a list. So, let's first initialize the chessboard size to the number of inner corners:

```
def _init_custom_layout(self):
    """Initializes camera calibration"""
    # setting chessboard size
    self.chessboard_size = (9, 6)
```

Next, we need to enumerate all the object points and assign them object point coordinates so that the first point has coordinates *(0,0)*, the second one (top row) has coordinates *(1,0)*, and the last one has coordinates *(8,5)*:

```
# prepare object points
self.objp = np.zeros((np.prod(self.chessboard_size), 3),
    dtype=np.float32)
self.objp[:, :2] = np.mgrid[0:self.chessboard_size[0],
    0:self.chessboard_size[1]].T.reshape(-1, 2)
```

We also need to keep track of whether we are currently recording the object and image points or not. We will initiate this process once the user clicks on the `self.button_calibrate` button. After that, the algorithm will try to detect a chessboard in all subsequent frames until a number of `self.record_min_num_frames` chessboards have been detected:

```
# prepare recording
self.recording = False
self.record_min_num_frames = 20
self._reset_recording()
```

Whenever the `self.button_calibrate` button is clicked on, we reset all the bookkeeping variables, disable the button, and start recording:

```
def _on_button_calibrate(self, event):
    self.button_calibrate.Disable()
    self.recording = True
    self._reset_recording()
```

Resetting the bookkeeping variables involves clearing the lists of recorded object and image points (`self.obj_points` and `self.img_points`) as well as resetting the number of detected chessboards (`self.recordCnt`) to 0:

```
def _reset_recording(self):
    self.record_cnt = 0
    self.obj_points = []
    self.img_points = []
```

Collecting image and object points

The `_process_frame` method is responsible for doing the hard work of the calibration technique. After the `self.button_calibrate` button has been clicked on, this method starts collecting data until a total of `self.record_min_num_frames` chessboards are detected:

```
def _process_frame(self, frame):
    """Processes each frame"""

    # if we are not recording, just display the frame
    if not self.recording:
        return frame

    # else we're recording
    img_gray = cv2.cvtColor(frame,
        cv2.COLOR_BGR2GRAY).astype(np.uint8)

    if self.record_cnt < self.record_min_num_frames:
        ret, corners = cv2.findChessboardCorners(img_gray,
            self.chessboard_size, None)
```

The `cv2.findChessboardCorners` function will parse a grayscale image (`img_gray`) to find a chessboard of size `self.chessboard_size`. If the image indeed contains a chessboard, the function will return true (`ret`) as well as a list of chessboard corners (`corners`).

Then, drawing the chessboard is straightforward:

```
if ret:
    cv2.drawChessboardCorners(frame,
        self.chessboard_size, corners, ret)
```

The result looks like this (drawing the chessboard corners in color for the effect):

We could now simply store the list of detected corners and move on to the next frame. However, in order to make the calibration as accurate as possible, OpenCV provides a function to refine the corner point measurement:

```
criteria = (cv2.TERM_CRITERIA_EPS +
        cv2.TERM_CRITERIA_MAX_ITER, 30, 0.01)
cv2.cornerSubPix(img_gray, corners, (9, 9), (-1, -1),
        criteria)
```

This will refine the coordinates of the detected corners to subpixel precision. Now we are ready to append the object and image points to the list and advance the frame counter:

```
self.obj_points.append(self.objp)
self.img_points.append(corners)
self.record_cnt += 1
```

Finding the camera matrix

Once we have collected enough data (that is, once `self.record_cnt` reaches the value of `self.record_min_num_frames`), the algorithm is ready to perform the calibration. This process can be performed with a single call to `cv2.calibrateCamera`:

```
else:
    print "Calibrating..."
    ret, K, dist, rvecs, tvecs =
        cv2.calibrateCamera(self.obj_points,
            self.img_points, (self.imgHeight, self.imgWidth),
            None, None)
```

The function returns `true` on success (`ret`), the intrinsic camera matrix (`K`), the distortion coefficients (`dist`), as well as two rotation and translation matrices (`rvecs` and `tvecs`). For now, we are mainly interested in the camera matrix and the distortion coefficients, because these will allow us to compensate for any imperfections of the internal camera hardware. We will simply print them on the console for easy inspection:

```
print "K=", K
print "dist=", dist
```

For example, the calibration of my laptop's webcam recovered the following values:

```
K= [[ 3.36696445e+03 0.00000000e+00 2.99109943e+02]
    [ 0.00000000e+00 3.29683922e+03 2.69436829e+02]
    [ 0.00000000e+00 0.00000000e+00 1.00000000e+00]]
dist= [[ 9.87991355e-01 -3.18446968e+02 9.56790602e-02
        -3.42530800e-02 4.87489304e+03]]
```

This tells us that the focal lengths of my webcam are `fx=3366.9644` pixels and `fy=3296.8392` pixels, with the optical center at `cx=299.1099` pixels and `cy=269.4368` pixels.

A good idea might be to double-check the accuracy of the calibration process. This can be done by projecting the object points onto the image using the recovered camera parameters so that we can compare them with the list of image points we collected with the `cv2.findChessboardCorners` function. If the two points are roughly the same, we know that the calibration was successful. Even better, we can calculate the mean error of the reconstruction by projecting every object point in the list:

```
mean_error = 0
for i in xrange(len(self.obj_points)):
    img_points2, _ = cv2.projectPoints(self.obj_points[i],
        rvecs[i], tvecs[i], K, dist)
```

```
    error = cv2.norm(self.img_points[i], img_points2,
        cv2.NORM_L2)/len(img_points2)
    mean_error += error

print "mean error=", {} pixels".format(mean_error)
```

Performing this check on my laptop's webcam resulted in a mean error of 0.95 pixels, which is fairly close to zero.

With the internal camera parameters recovered, we can now set out to take beautiful, undistorted pictures of the world, possibly from different viewpoints so that we can extract some structure from motion.

Setting up the app

Going forward, we will be using a famous open source dataset called `fountain-P11`. It depicts a Swiss fountain viewed from various angles. An example of this is shown in the following image:

The dataset consists of 11 high-resolution images and can be downloaded from `http://cvlabwww.epfl.ch/data/multiview/denseMVS.html`. Had we taken the pictures ourselves, we would have had to go through the entire camera calibration procedure to recover the intrinsic camera matrix and the distortion coefficients. Luckily, these parameters are known for the camera that took the fountain dataset, so we can go ahead and hardcode these values in our code.

The main function routine

Our main function routine will consist of creating and interacting with an instance of the `SceneReconstruction3D` class. This code can be found in the `chapter4.py` file, which imports all the necessary modules and instantiates the class:

```
import numpy as np

from scene3D import SceneReconstruction3D


def main():
    # camera matrix and distortion coefficients
    # can be recovered with calibrate.py
    # but the examples used here are already undistorted, taken
    # with a camera of known K
    K = np.array([[2759.48/4, 0, 1520.69/4, 0, 2764.16/4,
        1006.81/4, 0, 0, 1]]).reshape(3, 3)
    d = np.array([0.0, 0.0, 0.0, 0.0, 0.0]).reshape(1, 5)
```

Here, the K matrix is the intrinsic camera matrix for the camera that took the fountain dataset. According to the photographer, these images are already distortion free, so we set all the distortion coefficients (d) to zero.

Note that if you want to run the code presented in this chapter on a dataset other than `fountain-P11`, you will have to adjust the intrinsic camera matrix and the distortion coefficients.

Next, we load a pair of images to which we would like to apply our structure-from-motion techniques. I downloaded the dataset into a subdirectory called `fountain_dense`:

```
# load a pair of images for which to perform SfM
scene = SceneReconstruction3D(K, d)
scene.load_image_pair("fountain_dense/0004.png",
    "fountain_dense/0005.png")
```

Now we are ready to perform various computations, such as the following:

```
scene.plot_optic_flow()
scene.draw_epipolar_lines()
scene.plot_rectified_images()

# draw 3D point cloud of fountain
# use "pan axes" button in pyplot to inspect the cloud (rotate
# and zoom to convince you of the result)
scene.plot_point_cloud()
```

The next sections will explain these functions in detail.

The SceneReconstruction3D class

All of the relevant 3D scene reconstruction code for this chapter can be found as part of the SceneReconstruction3D class in the scene3D module. Upon instantiation, the class stores the intrinsic camera parameters to be used in all subsequent calculations:

```
import cv2
import numpy as np
import sys

from mpl_toolkits.mplot3d import Axes3D
import matplotlib.pyplot as plt


class SceneReconstruction3D:
    def __init__(self, K, dist):
        self.K = K
        self.K_inv = np.linalg.inv(K)
        self.d = dist
```

Then, the first step is to load a pair of images on which to operate:

```
def load_image_pair(self, img_path1, img_path2,
        downscale=True):
    self.img1 = cv2.imread(img_path1, cv2.CV_8UC3)
    self.img2 = cv2.imread(img_path2, cv2.CV_8UC3)

    # make sure images are valid
    if self.img1 is None:
        sys.exit("Image " + img_path1 + " could not be
            loaded.")
    if self.img2 is None:
        sys.exit("Image " + img_path2 + " could not be
            loaded.")
```

If the loaded images are grayscale, the method will convert to them to BGR format, because the other methods expect a three-channel image:

```
if len(self.img1.shape)==2:
    self.img1 = cv2.cvtColor(self.img1, cv2.COLOR_GRAY2BGR)
    self.img2 = cv2.cvtColor(self.img2, cv2.COLOR_GRAY2BGR)
```

In the case of the fountain sequence, all images are of a relatively high resolution. If an optional `downscale` flag is set, the method will downscale the images to a width of roughly 600 pixels:

```
# scale down image if necessary
# to something close to 600px wide
target_width = 600
if downscale and self.img1.shape[1]>target_width:
    while self.img1.shape[1] > 2*target_width:
        self.img1 = cv2.pyrDown(self.img1)
        self.img2 = cv2.pyrDown(self.img2)
```

Also, we need to compensate for the radial and tangential lens distortions using the distortion coefficients specified earlier (if there are any):

```
self.img1 = cv2.undistort(self.img1, self.K, self.d)
self.img2 = cv2.undistort(self.img2, self.K, self.d)
```

Finally, we are ready to move on to the meat of the project—estimating the camera motion and reconstructing the scene!

Estimating the camera motion from a pair of images

Now that we have loaded two images (`self.img1` and `self.img2`) of the same scene, such as two examples from the fountain dataset, we find ourselves in a similar situation as in the last chapter. We are given two images that supposedly show the same rigid object or static scene, but from different viewpoints. However, this time we want to go a step further; if the only thing that changes between taking the two pictures is the location of the camera, can we infer the relative camera motion by looking at the matching features?

Well, of course we can. Otherwise, this chapter would not make much sense, would it? We will take the location and orientation of the camera in the first image as a given and then find out how much we have to reorient and relocate the camera so that its viewpoint matches that from the second image.

In other words, we need to recover the **essential matrix** of the camera in the second image. An essential matrix is a 4 x 3 matrix that is the concatenation of a 3 x 3 rotation matrix and a 3 x 1 translation matrix. It is often denoted as [R | t]. You can think of it as capturing the position and orientation of the camera in the second image relative to the camera in the first image.

The crucial step in recovering the essential matrix (as well as all other transformations in this chapter) is feature matching. We can either reuse our code from the last chapter and apply a speeded-up robust features (SURF) detector to the two images, or calculate the optic flow between the two images. The user may choose their favorite method by specifying a feature extraction mode, which will be implemented by the following private method:

```python
def ___extract_keypoints(self, feat_mode):
    if featMode == "SURF":
        # feature matching via SURF and BFMatcher
        self._extract_keypoints_surf()
    else:
        if feat_mode == "flow":
            # feature matching via optic flow
            self._extract_keypoints_flow()
        else:
            sys.exit("Unknown mode " + feat_mode
                + ". Use 'SURF' or 'FLOW'")
```

Point matching using rich feature descriptors

As we saw in the last chapter, a fast and robust way of extracting important features from an image is by using a SURF detector. In this chapter, we want to use it for two images, `self.img1` and `self.img2`:

```python
def _extract_keypoints_surf(self):
    detector = cv2.SURF(250)
    first_key_points, first_des =
        detector.detectAndCompute(self.img1, None)
    second_key_points, second_desc =
        detector.detectAndCompute(self.img2, None)
```

For feature matching, we will use a `BruteForce` matcher, but other matchers (such as FLANN) can work as well:

```python
matcher = cv2.BFMatcher(cv2.NORM_L1, True)
matches = matcher.match(first_desc, second_desc)
```

For each of the matches, we need to recover the corresponding image coordinates. These are maintained in the `self.match_pts1` and `self.match_pts2` lists:

```
first_match_points = np.zeros((len(matches), 2),
    dtype=np.float32)
second_match_points = np.zeros_like(first_match_points)
for i in range(len(matches)):
    first_match_points[i] =
        first_key_points[matches[i].queryIdx].pt
    second_match_points[i] =
        second_key_points[matches[i].trainIdx].pt

self.match_pts1 = first_match_points
self.match_pts2 = second_match_points
```

The following screenshot shows an example of the feature matcher applied to two arbitrary frames of the fountain sequence:

Point matching using optic flow

An alternative to using rich features, is using optic flow. Optic flow is the process of estimating motion between two consecutive image frames by calculating a displacement vector. A displacement vector can be calculated for every pixel in the image (dense) or only for selected points (sparse).

One of the most commonly used techniques for calculating dense optic flow is the **Lukas-Kanade** method. It can be implemented in OpenCV with a single line of code, by using the `cv2.calcOpticalFlowPyrLK` function.

But before that, we need to select some points in the image that are worth tracking. Again, this is a question of feature selection. If we were interested in getting an exact result for only a few highly salient image points, we can use Shi-Tomasi's `cv2.goodFeaturesToTrack` function. This function might recover features like this:

However, in order to infer structure from motion, we might need many more features and not just the most salient Harris corners. An alternative would be to detect the FAST features:

```
def _extract_keypoints_flow(self):
    fast = cv2.FastFeatureDetector()
    first_key_points = fast.detect(self.img1, None)
```

We can then calculate the optic flow for these features. In other words, we want to find the points in the second image that most likely correspond to the `first_key_points` from the first image. For this, we need to convert the keypoint list into a NumPy array of `(x,y)` coordinates:

```
first_key_list = [i.pt for i in first_key_points]
first_key_arr = np.array(first_key_list).astype(np.float32)
```

Then the optic flow will return a list of corresponding features in the second image (`second_key_arr`):

```
second_key_arr, status, err =
    cv2.calcOpticalFlowPyrLK(self.img1, self.img2,
        first_key_arr)
```

The function also returns a vector of status bits (`status`), which indicate whether the flow for a keypoint has been found or not, and a vector of estimated error values (`err`). If we were to ignore these two additional vectors, the recovered flow field could look something like this:

In this image, an arrow is drawn for each keypoint, starting at the image location of the keypoint in the first image and pointing to the image location of the same keypoint in the second image. By inspecting the flow image, we can see that the camera moved mostly to the right, but there also seems to be a rotational component. However, some of these arrows are really large, and some of them make no sense. For example, it is very unlikely that a pixel in the bottom-right image corner actually moved all the way to the top of the image. It is much more likely that the flow calculation for this particular keypoint is wrong. Thus, we want to exclude all the keypoints for which the status bit is zero or the estimated error is larger than some value:

```
condition = (status == 1) * (err < 5.)
concat = np.concatenate((condition, condition), axis=1)
first_match_points = first_key_arr[concat].reshape(-1, 2)
second_match_points = second_key_arr[concat].reshape(-1, 2)

self.match_pts1 = first_match_points
self.match_pts2 = second_match_points
```

If we draw the flow field again with a limited set of keypoints, the image will look like this:

The flow field can be drawn with the following public method, which first extracts the keypoints using the preceding code and then draws the actual lines on the image:

```
def plot_optic_flow(self):
    self._extract_key_points("flow")

    img = self.img1
    for i in xrange(len(self.match_pts1)):
        cv2.line(img, tuple(self.match_pts1[i]),
            tuple(self.match_pts2[i]), color=(255, 0, 0))
        theta = np.arctan2(self.match_pts2[i][1] -
            self.match_pts1[i][1], self.match_pts2[i][0] -
            self.match_pts1[i][0])
        cv2.line(img, tuple(self.match_pts2[i]),
            (np.int(self.match_pts2[i][0] -
            6*np.cos(theta+np.pi/4)),
            np.int(self.match_pts2[i][1] -
            6*np.sin(theta+np.pi/4))), color=(255, 0, 0))
        cv2.line(img, tuple(self.match_pts2[i]),
            (np.int(self.match_pts2[i][0] -
            6*np.cos(theta-np.pi/4)),
```

```
            np.int(self.match_pts2[i][1] -
            6*np.sin(theta-np.pi/4))), color=(255, 0, 0))
    for i in xrange(len(self.match_pts1)):
        cv2.line(img, tuple(self.match_pts1[i]),
            tuple(self.match_pts2[i]), color=(255, 0, 0))
        theta = np.arctan2(self.match_pts2[i][1] -
            self.match_pts1[i][1],
            self.match_pts2[i][0] - self.match_pts1[i][0])
    cv2.imshow("imgFlow",img)
    cv2.waitKey()
```

The advantage of using optic flow instead of rich features is that the process is usually faster and can accommodate the matching of many more points, making the reconstruction denser.

The caveat in working with optic flow is that it works best for consecutive images taken by the same hardware, whereas rich features are mostly agnostic to this.

Finding the camera matrices

Now that we have obtained the matches between keypoints, we can calculate two important camera matrices: the fundamental matrix and the essential matrix. These matrices will specify the camera motion in terms of rotational and translational components. Obtaining the fundamental matrix (self.F) is another OpenCV one-liner:

```
def _find_fundamental_matrix(self):
    self.F, self.Fmask = cv2.findFundamentalMat(self.match_pts1,
        self.match_pts2, cv2.FM_RANSAC, 0.1, 0.99)
```

The only difference between the fundamental matrix and the essential matrix is that the latter operates on rectified images:

```
def _find_essential_matrix(self):
    self.E = self.K.T.dot(self.F).dot(self.K)
```

The essential matrix (self.E) can then be decomposed into rotational and translational components, denoted as [R | t], using **singular value decomposition (SVD)**:

```
def _find_camera_matrices(self):
    U, S, Vt = np.linalg.svd(self.E)
    W = np.array([0.0, -1.0, 0.0, 1.0, 0.0, 0.0, 0.0, 0.0,
        1.0]).reshape(3, 3)
```

Using the unitary matrices U and V in combination with an additional matrix, W, we can now reconstruct [R | t]. However, it can be shown that this decomposition has four possible solutions and only one of them is the valid second camera matrix. The only thing we can do is check all four possible solutions and find the one that predicts that all the imaged keypoints lie in front of both cameras.

But prior to that, we need to convert the keypoints from 2D image coordinates to homogeneous coordinates. We achieve this by adding a z coordinate, which we set to 1:

```
first_inliers = []
second_inliers = []
for i in range(len(self.Fmask)):
    if self.Fmask[i]:
        first_inliers.append(self.K_inv.dot(
            [self.match_pts1[i][0], self.match_pts1[i][1],
            1.0]))
        second_inliers.append(self.K_inv.dot(
            [self.match_pts2[i][0], self.match_pts2[i][1],
            1.0]))
```

We then iterate over the four possible solutions and choose the one that has _in_ front_of_both_cameras **returning** True:

```
# First choice: R = U * Wt * Vt, T = +u_3 (See Hartley
# & Zisserman 9.19)
R = U.dot(W).dot(Vt)
T = U[:, 2]

if not self._in_front_of_both_cameras(first_inliers,
        second_inliers, R, T):
    # Second choice: R = U * W * Vt, T = -u_3
    T = - U[:, 2]

if not self._in_front_of_both_cameras(first_inliers,
        second_inliers, R, T):
    # Third choice: R = U * Wt * Vt, T = u_3
    R = U.dot(W.T).dot(Vt)
    T = U[:, 2]

if not self._in_front_of_both_cameras(first_inliers,
        second_inliers, R, T):
    # Fourth choice: R = U * Wt * Vt, T = -u_3
    T = - U[:, 2]
```

Now, we can finally construct the [R | t] matrices of the two cameras. The first camera is simply a canonical camera (no translation and no rotation):

```
self.Rt1 = np.hstack((np.eye(3), np.zeros((3, 1))))
```

The second camera matrix consists of [R | t] recovered earlier:

```
self.Rt2 = np.hstack((R, T.reshape(3, 1)))
```

The __InFrontOfBothCameras private method is a helper function that makes sure that every pair of keypoints is mapped to 3D coordinates that make them lie in front of both cameras:

```
def _in_front_of_both_cameras(self, first_points, second_points,
        rot, trans):
    rot_inv = rot
    for first, second in zip(first_points, second_points):
        first_z = np.dot(rot[0, :] - second[0]*rot[2, :], trans) /
            np.dot(rot[0, :] - second[0]*rot[2, :], second)
        first_3d_point = np.array([first[0] * first_z, second[0] *
            first_z, first_z])
        second_3d_point = np.dot(rot.T, first_3d_point) -
            np.dot(rot.T, trans)
```

If the function finds any keypoint that is not in front of both cameras, it will return False:

```
if first_3d_point[2] < 0 or second_3d_point[2] < 0:
    return False
return True
```

Image rectification

Maybe, the easiest way to make sure that we have recovered the correct camera matrices is to rectify the images. If they are rectified correctly, then; a point in the first image, and a point in the second image that correspond to the same 3D world point, will lie on the same vertical coordinate. In a more concrete example, such as in our case, since we know that the cameras are upright, we can verify that horizontal lines in the rectified image correspond to horizontal lines in the 3D scene.

First, we perform all the steps described in the previous subsections to obtain the [R | t] matrix of the second camera:

```
def plot_rectified_images(self, feat_mode="SURF"):
    self._extract_keypoints(feat_mode)
    self._find_fundamental_matrix()
    self._find_essential_matrix()
```

```
self._find_camera_matrices_rt()

R = self.Rt2[:, :3]
T = self.Rt2[:, 3]
```

Then, rectification can be performed with two OpenCV one-liners that remap the image coordinates to the rectified coordinates based on the camera matrix (self.K), the distortion coefficients (self.d), the rotational component of the essential matrix (R), and the translational component of the essential matrix (T):

```
R1, R2, P1, P2, Q, roi1, roi2 = cv2.stereoRectify(self.K,
    self.d, self.K, self.d, self.img1.shape[:2], R, T,
    alpha=1.0)
mapx1, mapy1 = cv2.initUndistortRectifyMap(self.K,
    self.d, R1, self.K, self.img1.shape[:2], cv2.CV_32F)
mapx2, mapy2 = cv2.initUndistortRectifyMap(self.K, self.d, R2,
    self.K, self.img2.shape[:2], cv2.CV_32F)
img_rect1 = cv2.remap(self.img1, mapx1, mapy1,
    cv2.INTER_LINEAR)
img_rect2 = cv2.remap(self.img2, mapx2, mapy2,
    cv2.INTER_LINEAR)
```

To make sure that the rectification is accurate, we plot the two rectified images (img_rect1 and img_rect2) next to each other:

```
total_size = (max(img_rect1.shape[0], img_rect2.shape[0]),
    img_rect1.shape[1] + img_rect2.shape[1], 3)
img = np.zeros(total_size, dtype=np.uint8)
img[:img_rect1.shape[0], :img_rect1.shape[1]] = img_rect1
img[:img_rect2.shape[0], img_rect1.shape[1]:] = img_rect2
```

We also draw horizontal blue lines after every 25 pixels, across the side-by-side images to further help us visually investigate the rectification process:

```
for i in range(20, img.shape[0], 25):
    cv2.line(img, (0, i), (img.shape[1], i), (255, 0, 0))
    cv2.imshow('imgRectified', img)
```

Now we can easily convince ourselves that the rectification was successful,
as shown here:

Reconstructing the scene

Finally, we can reconstruct the 3D scene by making use of a process called
triangulation. We are able to infer the 3D coordinates of a point because of the
way **epipolar geometry** works. By calculating the essential matrix, we get to know
more about the geometry of the visual scene than we might think. Because the two
cameras depict the same real-world scene, we know that most of the 3D real-world
points will be found in both images. Moreover, we know that the mapping from the
2D image points to the corresponding 3D real-world points, will follow the rules of
geometry. If we study a sufficiently large number of image points, we can construct,
and solve, a (large) system of linear equations to get the ground truth of the real-
world coordinates.

Let's return to the Swiss fountain dataset. If we ask two photographers to take a picture of the fountain from different viewpoints at the same time, it is not hard to realize that the first photographer might show up in the picture of the second photographer, and vice-versa. The point on the image plane where the other photographer is visible is called the **epipole** or **epipolar point**. In more technical terms, the epipole is the point on one camera's image plane onto which the center of projection of the other camera projects. It is interesting to note that both the epipoles in their respective image planes, and both the centers of projection, lie on a single 3D line. By looking at the lines between the epipoles and image points, we can limit the number of possible 3D coordinates of the image points. In fact, if the projection point is known, then the epipolar line (which is the line between the image point and the epipole) is known, and in turn the same point projected onto the second image must lie on that particular epipolar line. Confusing? I thought so. Let's just look at these images:

Each line here is the epipolar line of a particular point in the image. Ideally, all the epipolar lines drawn in the left-hand-side image should intersect at a point, and that point typically lies outside the image. If the calculation is accurate, then that point should coincide with the location of the second camera as seen from the first camera. In other words, the epipolar lines in the left-hand-side image tell us that the camera that took the right-hand-side image is located to our (that is, the first camera's) right-hand side. Analogously, the epipolar lines in the right-hand-side image tell us that the camera that took the image on the left is located to our (that is, the second camera's) left-hand side.

Moreover, for each point observed in one image, the same point must be observed in the other image on a known epipolar line. This is known as **epipolar constraint**. We can use this fact to show that if two image points correspond to the same 3D point, then the projection lines of those two image points must intersect precisely at the 3D point. This means that the 3D point can be calculated from two image points, which is what we are going to do next.

Luckily, OpenCV again provides a wrapper to solve an extensive set of linear equations. First, we have to convert our list of matching feature points into a NumPy array:

```
first_inliers = np.array(self.match_inliers1).reshape
    (-1, 3)[:, :2]
second_inliers = np.array(self.match_inliers2).reshape
    (-1, 3)[:, :2]
```

Triangulation is performed next, using the preceding two [R | t] matrices (`self.Rt1` for the first camera and `self.Rt2` for the second camera):

```
pts4D = cv2.triangulatePoints(self.Rt1, self.Rt2, first_inliers.T,
    second_inliers.T).T
```

This will return the triangulated real-world points using 4D homogeneous coordinates. To convert them to 3D coordinates, we need to divide the *(X,Y,Z)* coordinates by the fourth coordinate, usually referred to as *W*:

```
pts3D = pts4D[:, :3]/np.repeat(pts4D[:, 3], 3).reshape(-1, 3)
```

3D point cloud visualization

The last step is visualizing the triangulated 3D real-world points. An easy way of creating 3D scatterplots is by using matplotlib. However, if you are looking for more professional visualization tools, you may be interested in Mayavi (`http://docs.enthought.com/mayavi/mayavi`), VisPy (`http://vispy.org`), or the Point Cloud Library (`http://pointclouds.org`). Although the latter does not have Python support for point cloud visualization yet, it is an excellent tool for point cloud segmentation, filtering, and sample consensus model fitting. For more information, head over to strawlab's GitHub repository at `https://github.com/strawlab/python-pcl`.

Before we can plot our 3D point cloud, we obviously have to extract the [R | t] matrix and perform the triangulation as explained earlier:

```
def plot_point_cloud(self, feat_mode="SURF"):
    self._extract_keypoints(feat_mode)
    self._find_fundamental_matrix()
    self._find_essential_matrix()
    self._find_camera_matrices_rt()

    # triangulate points
    first_inliers = np.array(
        self.match_inliers1).reshape(-1, 3)[:, :2]
```

```
second_inliers = np.array(
    self.match_inliers2).reshape(-1, 3)[:, :2]
pts4D = cv2.triangulatePoints(self.Rt1, self.Rt2,
    first_inliers.T, second_inliers.T).T

# convert from homogeneous coordinates to 3D
pts3D = pts4D[:, :3]/np.repeat(pts4D[:, 3], 3).reshape(-1, 3)
```

Then, all we need to do is open a `matplotlib` figure and draw each entry of `pts3D` in a 3D scatterplot:

```
Ys = pts3D[:,0]
Zs = pts3D[:,1]
Xs = pts3D[:,2]

fig = plt.figure()
ax = fig.add_subplot(111, projection='3d')
ax.scatter(Xs, Ys, Zs, c='r', marker='o')
ax.set_xlabel('Y')
ax.set_ylabel('Z')
ax.set_zlabel('X')
plt.show()
```

The result is most compelling when studied using pyplot's **Pan axes** button, which lets you rotate and scale the point cloud in all three dimensions. This will make it immediately clear that most of the points that you see lie on the same plane, namely the wall behind the fountain, and that the fountain itself extends from that wall in negative z coordinates. It is a little harder to draw this convincingly, but here we go:

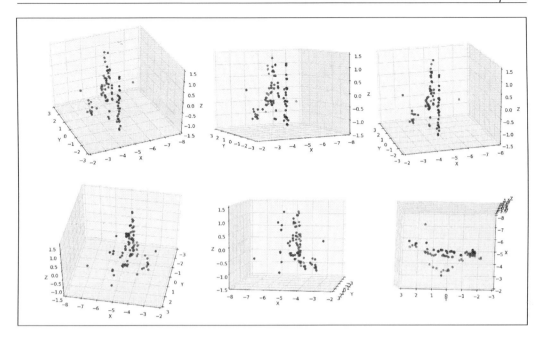

Each subplot shows the recovered 3D coordinates of the fountain as seen from a different angle. In the top row, we are looking at the fountain from a similar angle as the second camera in the previous images, that is, by standing to the right and slightly in front of the fountain. You can see how most of the points are mapped to a similar x coordinate, which corresponds to the wall behind the fountain. For a subset of points concentrated between z coordinates *-0.5* and *-1.0*, the x coordinate is significantly different, which shows different keypoints that belong to the surface of the fountain. The first two panels in the lower row look at the fountain from the other side. The last panel shows a birds-eye view of the fountain, highlighting the fountain's silhouette as a half-circle in the lower half of the image.

Summary

In this chapter, we explored a way of reconstructing a scene in 3D—by inferring the geometrical features of 2D images taken by the same camera. We wrote a script to calibrate a camera, and you learned about fundamental and essential matrices. We used this knowledge to perform triangulation. We then went on to visualize the real-world geometry of the scene in a 3D point cloud. Using simple 3D scatterplots in matplotlib, we found a way to convince ourselves that our calculations were accurate and practical.

Going forward from here, it will be possible to store the triangulated 3D points in a file that can be parsed by the Point Cloud Library, or to repeat the procedure for different image pairs so that we can generate a denser and more accurate reconstruction. Although we have covered a lot in this chapter, there is a lot more left to do. Typically, when talking about a structure-from-motion pipeline, we include two additional steps that we have not talked about so far: bundle adjustment and geometry fitting. One of the most important steps in such a pipeline is to refine the 3D estimate in order to minimize reconstruction errors. Typically, we would also want to get all points that do not belong to our object of interest out of the cloud. But with the basic code in hand, you can now go ahead and write your own advanced structure-from-motion pipeline!

In the next chapter, we will move away from rigid scenes and instead focus on tracking visually salient and moving objects in a scene. This will give you an understanding of how to deal with non-static scenes. We will also explore how we can make an algorithm focus on *what's important* in a scene, quickly, which is a technique known to speed up object detection, object recognition, object tracking, and content-aware image editing.

5
Tracking Visually Salient Objects

The goal of this chapter is to track multiple visually salient objects in a video sequence at once. Instead of labeling the objects of interest in the video ourselves, we will let the algorithm decide which regions of a video frame are worth tracking.

We have previously learned how to detect simple objects of interest (such as a human hand) in tightly controlled scenarios or how to infer geometrical features of a visual scene from camera motion. In this chapter, we ask what we can learn about a visual scene by looking at the **image statistics** of a large number of frames. By analyzing the **Fourier spectrum** of natural images we will build a **saliency map**, which allows us to label certain statistically interesting patches of the image as (potential or) *proto-objects*. We will then feed the location of all the proto- objects to a **mean-shift tracker** that will allow us to keep track of where the objects move from one frame to the next.

To build the app, we need to combine the following two main features:

- **Saliency map**: We will use Fourier analysis to get a general understanding of natural image statistics, which will help us build a model of what general image backgrounds look like. By comparing and contrasting the background model to a specific image frame, we can locate sub-regions of the image that *pop out* of their surroundings. Ideally, these sub-regions correspond to the image patches that tend to grab our immediate attention when looking at the image.

- **Object tracking**: Once all the potentially *interesting* patches of an image are located, we will track their movement over many frames using a simple yet effective method called mean-shift tracking. Because it is possible to have multiple proto-objects in the scene that might change appearance over time, we need to be able to distinguish between them and keep track of all of them.

Visual saliency is a technical term from cognitive psychology that tries to describe the visual quality of certain objects or items that allows them to grab our immediate attention. Our brains constantly drive our gaze towards the *important* regions of the visual scene and keep track of them over time, allowing us to quickly scan our surroundings for interesting objects and events while neglecting the less important parts.

An example of a regular RGB image and its conversion to a saliency map, where the statistically interesting *pop-out* regions appear bright and the others dark, is shown in the following figure:

Traditional models might try to associate particular features with each target (much like our feature matching approach in *Chapter 3, Finding Objects via Feature Matching and Perspective Transforms*), which would convert the problem to the detection of specific categories or objects. However, these models require manual labeling and training. But what if the features or the number of the objects to track is not known?

Instead, we will try to mimic what the brain does, that is, tune our algorithm to the statistics of the natural images, so that we can immediately locate the patterns or sub-regions that "grab our attention" in the visual scene (that is, patterns that deviate from these statistical regularities) and flag them for further inspection. The result is an algorithm that works for any number of proto-objects in the scene, such as tracking all the players on a soccer field. Refer to the following image:

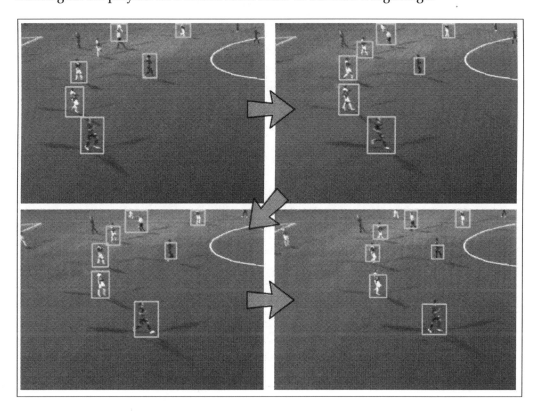

This chapter uses OpenCV 2.4.9, as well as the additional packages NumPy (http://www.numpy.org), wxPython 2.8 (http://www.wxpython.org/download.php), and matplotlib (http://www.matplotlib.org/downloads.html). Although parts of the algorithms presented in this chapter have been added to an optional Saliency module of the OpenCV 3.0.0 release, there is currently no Python API for it, so we will write our own code.

Planning the app

The final app will convert each RGB frame of a video sequence into a saliency map, extract all the interesting proto-objects, and feed them to a mean-shift tracking algorithm. To do this, we need the following components:

- `main`: The main function routine (in `chapter5.py`) to start the application.

- `Saliency`: A class that generates a saliency map from an RGB color image. It includes the following public methods:

  - `Saliency.get_saliency_map`: The main method to convert an RGB color image to a saliency map

  - `Saliency.get_proto_objects_map`: A method to convert a saliency map into a binary mask containing all the proto-objects

  - `Saliency.plot_power_density`: A method to display the 2D power density of an RGB color image, which is helpful to understand the Fourier transform

  - `Saliency.plot_power_spectrum`: A method to display the radially averaged power spectrum of an RGB color image, which is helpful to understand natural image statistics

- `MultiObjectTracker`: A class that tracks multiple objects in a video using mean-shift tracking. It includes the following public method, which itself contains a number of private helper methods:

  - `MultiObjectTracker.advance_frame`: A method to update the tracking information for a new frame, combining bounding boxes obtained from both the saliency map and mean-shift tracking

In the following sections, we will discuss these steps in detail.

Setting up the app

In order to run our app, we will need to execute a main function routine that reads a frame of a video stream, generates a saliency map, extracts the location of the proto-objects, and tracks these locations from one frame to the next.

The main function routine

The main process flow is handled by the main function in `chapter5.py`, which instantiates the two classes (`Saliency` and `MultipleObjectTracker`) and opens a video file showing the number of soccer players on the field:

```python
import cv2
import numpy as np
from os import path

from saliency import Saliency
from tracking import MultipleObjectsTracker


def main(video_file='soccer.avi', roi=((140, 100), (500, 600))):
    if path.isfile(video_file):
        video = cv2.VideoCapture(video_file)
    else:
        print 'File "' + video_file + '" does not exist.'
        raise SystemExit

    # initialize tracker
    mot = MultipleObjectsTracker()
```

The function will then read the video frame by frame, extract some meaningful region of interest (for illustration purposes), and feed it to the Saliency module:

```python
while True:
    success, img = video.read()
    if success:
        if roi:
            # grab some meaningful ROI
            img = img[roi[0][0]:roi[1][0],
                roi[0][1]:roi[1][1]]
        # generate saliency map
        sal = Saliency(img, use_numpy_fft=False,
            gauss_kernel=(3, 3))
```

The Saliency will generate a map of all the *interesting* proto-objects and feed that into the tracker module. The output of the tracker module is the input frame annotated with bounding boxes as shown in the preceding figure.

```python
cv2.imshow("tracker", mot.advance_frame(img,
        sal.get_proto_objects_map(use_otsu=False)))
```

The app will run through all the frames of the video until the end of the file is reached or the user presses the *q* key:

```
if cv2.waitKey(100) & 0xFF == ord('q'):
    break
```

The Saliency class

The constructor of the Saliency class accepts a video frame, which can be either grayscale or RGB, as well as some options such as whether to use NumPy's or OpenCV's Fourier package:

```
def __init__(self, img, use_numpy_fft=True, gauss_kernel=(5, 5)):
    self.use_numpy_fft = use_numpy_fft
    self.gauss_kernel = gauss_kernel
    self.frame_orig = img
```

A saliency map will be generated from a down sampled version of the image, and because the computation is relatively time-intensive, we will maintain a flag need_saliency_map that makes sure we do the computations only once:

```
    self.small_shape = (64, 64)
    self.frame_small = cv2.resize(img, self.small_shape[1::-1])

    # whether we need to do the math (True) or it has already
    # been done (False)
    self.need_saliency_map = True
```

From then on, the user may call any of the class' public methods, which will all be passed on the same image.

The MultiObjectTracker class

The constructor of the tracker class is straightforward. All it does is set up the termination criteria for mean-shift tracking and store the conditions for the minimum contour area (min_area) and minimum frame-by-frame drift (min_shift2) to be considered in the subsequent computation steps:

```
def __init__(self, min_area=400, min_shift2=5):
    self.object_roi = []
    self.object_box = []

    self.min_cnt_area = min_area
    self.min_shift2 = min_shift2

    # Setup the termination criteria, either 100 iteration or move
    # by at least 1 pt
    self.term_crit = (cv2.TERM_CRITERIA_EPS |
        cv2.TERM_CRITERIA_COUNT, 100, 1)
```

From then on, the user may call the `advance_frame` method to feed a new frame to the tracker.

However, before we make use of all this functionality, we need to learn about image statistics and how to generate a saliency map.

Visual saliency

As already mentioned in the introduction, visual saliency tries to describe the visual quality of certain objects or items that allows them to grab our immediate attention. Our brains constantly drive our gaze towards the *important* regions of the visual scene, as if it were to shine a flashlight on different sub-regions of the visual world, allowing us to quickly scan our surroundings for interesting objects and events while neglecting the less important parts.

It is thought that this is an evolutionary strategy to deal with the constant **information overflow** that comes with living in a visually rich environment. For example, if you take a casual walk through a jungle, you want to be able to notice the attacking tiger in the bush to your left before admiring the intricate color pattern on the butterfly's wings in front of you. As a result, the visually salient objects have the remarkable quality of *popping out* of their surroundings, much like the target bars in the following figure:

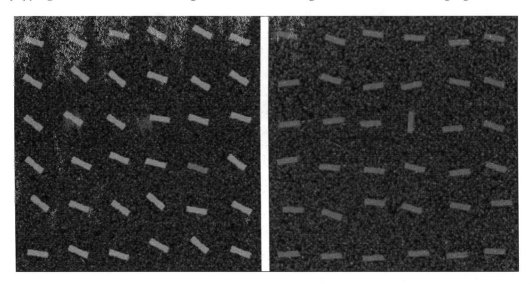

The visual quality that makes these targets pop out may not always be trivial though. If you are viewing the image on the left in color, you may immediately notice the only red bar in the image. However, if you look at the same image in grayscale, the target bar will be hard to find (it is the fourth bar from the top, fifth bar from the left). Similar to color saliency, there is a visually salient bar in the image on the right. Although the target bar is of unique color in the left image and of unique orientation in the right image, put the two characteristics together and suddenly the unique target bar does not pop out anymore:

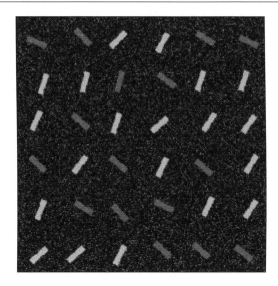

In this preceding display, there is again one bar that is unique and different from all the other ones. However, because of the way the distracting items were designed, there is little salience to guide you towards the target bar. Instead, you find yourself scanning the image, seemingly at random, looking for something interesting. (Hint: The target is the only red and almost-vertical bar in the image, second row from the top, third column from the left.)

What does this have to do with computer vision, you ask? Quite a lot, actually. Artificial vision systems suffer from information overload much like you and me, except that they know even less about the world than we do. What if we could extract some insights from biology and use them to teach our algorithms something about the world? Imagine a dashboard camera in your car that automatically focuses on the most relevant traffic sign. Imagine a surveillance camera that is part of a wildlife observation station that will automatically detect and track the sighting of the notoriously shy platypus but will ignore everything else. How can we teach the algorithm what is important and what is not? How can we make that platypus "pop out"?

Fourier analysis

To find the visually salient sub-regions of an image, we need to look at its **frequency spectrum**. So far we have treated all our images and video frames in the **spatial domain**; that is, by analyzing the pixels or studying how the image intensity changes in different sub-regions of the image. However, the images can also be represented in the **frequency domain**; that is, by analyzing the pixel frequencies or studying how often and with what periodicity the pixels show up in the image.

An image can be transformed from the space domain into the frequency domain by applying the **Fourier transform**. In the frequency domain, we no longer think in terms of image coordinates *(x,y)*. Instead, we aim to find the spectrum of an image. Fourier's radical idea basically boils down to the following question: what if any signal or image could be transformed into a series of circular paths (also called **harmonics**)?

For example, think of a rainbow. Beautiful, isn't it? In a rainbow, white sunlight (composed of many different colors or parts of the spectrum) is spread into its spectrum. Here the color spectrum of the sunlight is exposed when the rays of light pass through raindrops (much like white light passing through a glass prism). The Fourier transform aims to do the same thing: to recover all the different parts of the spectrum that are contained in the sunlight.

A similar thing can be achieved for arbitrary images. In contrast to rainbows, where frequency corresponds to electromagnetic frequency, with images we consider spatial frequency; that is, the spatial periodicity of the pixel values. In an image of a prison cell, you can think of spatial frequency as (the inverse of) the distance between two adjacent prison bars.

The insights that can be gained from this change of perspective are very powerful. Without going into too much detail, let us just remark that a Fourier spectrum comes with both a magnitude and a phase. While the magnitude describes the amount of different frequencies in the image, the phase talks about the spatial location of these frequencies. The following image shows a natural image on the left and the corresponding Fourier magnitude spectrum (of the grayscale version) on the right:

The magnitude spectrum on the right tells us which frequency components are the most prominent (bright) in the grayscale version of the image on the left. The spectrum is adjusted so that the center of the image corresponds to zero frequency in x and y. The further you move to the border of the image, the higher the frequency gets. This particular spectrum is telling us that there are a lot of low-frequency components in the image on the left (clustered around the center of the image).

In OpenCV, this transformation can be achieved with the **Discrete Fourier Transform (DFT)** using the `plot_magnitude` method of the `Saliency` class. The procedure is as follows:

1. **Convert the image to grayscale if necessary**: Because the method accepts both grayscale and RGB color images, we need to make sure we operate on a single-channel image:

```python
def plot_magnitude(self):
    if len(self.frame_orig.shape)>2:
        frame = cv2.cvtColor(self.frame_orig,
            cv2.COLOR_BGR2GRAY)
    else:
        frame = self.frame_orig
```

2. **Expand the image to an optimal size**: It turns out that the performance of a DFT depends on the image size. It tends to be fastest for the image sizes that are multiples of the number two. It is therefore generally a good idea to pad the image with zeros:

```python
rows, cols = self.frame_orig.shape[:2]
nrows = cv2.getOptimalDFTSize(rows)
ncols = cv2.getOptimalDFTSize(cols)
frame = cv2.copyMakeBorder(frame, 0, ncols-cols, 0,
    nrows-rows, cv2.BORDER_CONSTANT, value = 0)
```

3. **Apply the DFT**: This is a single function call in NumPy. The result is a 2D matrix of complex numbers:

```python
img_dft = np.fft.fft2(frame)
```

4. **Transform the real and complex values to magnitude**: A complex number has a real (Re) and a complex (imaginary - Im) part. To extract the magnitude, we take the absolute value:

```python
magn = np.abs(img_dft)
```

5. **Switch to a logarithmic scale**: It turns out that the dynamic range of the Fourier coefficients is usually too large to be displayed on the screen. We have some small and some high changing values that we can't observe like this. Therefore, the high values will all turn out as white points, and the small ones as black points. To use the gray scale values for visualization, we can transform our linear scale to a logarithmic one:

```python
log_magn = np.log10(magn)
```

6. **Shift quadrants**: To center the spectrum on the image. This makes it easier to visually inspect the magnitude spectrum:

```python
spectrum = np.fft.fftshift(log_magn)
```

7. **Return the result for plotting**:

```
return spectrum/np.max(spectrum)*255
```

Natural scene statistics

The human brain figured out how to focus on visually salient objects a long time ago. The natural world in which we live has some statistical regularities that makes it uniquely *natural*, as opposed to a chessboard pattern or a random company logo. Probably, the most commonly known statistical regularity is the 1/f law. It states that the amplitude of the ensemble of natural images obeys a 1/f distribution, as shown in the figure later This is sometimes also referred to as **scale invariance**.

A 1D power spectrum (as a function of frequency) of a 2D image can be visualized with the `plot_power_spectrum` method of the `Saliency` class. We can use a similar recipe as for the magnitude spectrum used previously, but we will have to make sure that we correctly collapse the 2D spectrum onto a single axis.

1. Convert the image to grayscale if necessary (same as earlier):

```
def plot_power_spectrum(self):
    if len(self.frame_orig.shape)>2:
        frame = cv2.cvtColor(self.frame_orig,
            cv2.COLOR_BGR2GRAY)
    else:
        frame = self.frame_orig
```

2. Expand the image to optimal size (same as earlier):

```
rows, cols = self.frame_orig.shape[:2]
nrows = cv2.getOptimalDFTSize(rows)
ncols = cv2.getOptimalDFTSize(cols)
frame = cv2.copyMakeBorder(frame, 0, ncols-cols, 0,
    nrows-rows, cv2.BORDER_CONSTANT, value = 0)
```

3. **Apply the DFT and get the log spectrum**: Here we give the user an option (via flag `use_numpy_fft`) to use either NumPy's or OpenCV's Fourier tools:

```
if self.use_numpy_fft:
    img_dft = np.fft.fft2(frame)
    spectrum = np.log10(np.real(np.abs(img_dft))**2)
else:
    img_dft = cv2.dft(np.float32(frame),
        flags=cv2.DFT_COMPLEX_OUTPUT)
    spectrum = np.log10(img_dft[:,:,0]**2
        + img_dft[:,:,1]**2)
```

4. **Perform radial averaging**: This is the tricky part. It would be wrong to simply average the 2D spectrum in the direction of x or y. What we are interested in is a spectrum as a function of frequency, independent of the exact orientation. This is sometimes also called the **radially averaged power spectrum (RAPS)**, and can be achieved by summing up all the frequency magnitudes, starting at the center of the image, looking into all possible (radial) directions, from some frequency r to r+dr. We use the binning function of NumPy's histogram to sum up the numbers, and accumulate them in the variable `histo`:

```
L = max(frame.shape)
freqs = np.fft.fftfreq(L)[:L/2]
dists = np.sqrt(np.fft.fftfreq(frame.shape[0])
    [:,np.newaxis]**2 + np.fft.fftfreq
        (frame.shape[1])**2)
dcount = np.histogram(dists.ravel(), bins=freqs)[0]
histo, bins = np.histogram(dists.ravel(), bins=freqs,
    weights=spectrum.ravel())
```

5. **Plot the result**: Finally, we can plot the accumulated numbers in histo, but must not forget to normalize these by the bin size (dcount):

```
centers = (bins[:-1] + bins[1:]) / 2
plt.plot(centers, histo/dcount)
plt.xlabel('frequency')
plt.ylabel('log-spectrum')
plt.show()
```

The result is a function that is inversely proportional to the frequency. If you want to be absolutely certain of the 1/f property, you could take `np.log10` of all the x values and make sure the curve is decreasing roughly linearly. On a linear x axis and logarithmic y axis, the plot looks like the following:

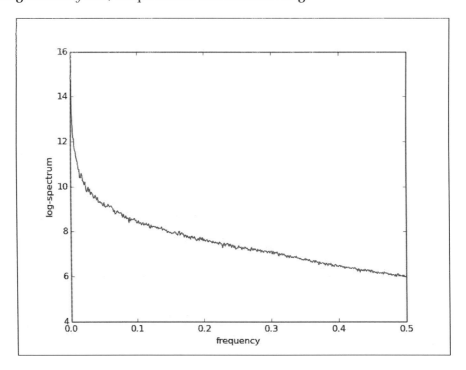

This property is quite remarkable. It states that if we were to average all the spectra of all the images ever taken of natural scenes (neglecting all the ones taken with fancy image filters, of course), we would get a curve that would look remarkably like the one shown in the preceding image.

But going back to the image of a peaceful little boat on the Limmat river, what about single images? We have just looked at the power spectrum of this image and witnessed the 1/f property. How can we use our knowledge of natural image statistics to tell an algorithm not to stare at the tree on the left, but instead focus on the boat that is chugging in the water?

This is where we realize what saliency really means.

Generating a Saliency map with the spectral residual approach

The things that deserve our attention in an image are not the image patches that follow the 1/f law, but the patches that stick out of the smooth curves. In other words, the statistical anomalies. These anomalies are termed the **spectral residual** of an image, and correspond to the potentially *interesting* patches of an image (or proto-objects). A map that shows these statistical anomalies as bright spots is called a saliency map.

The spectral residual approach described here is based on the original scientific publication by *Xiaodi Hou* and *Liqing Zhang* (2007). *Saliency Detection: A Spectral Residual Approach*. IEEE Transactions on Computer Vision and Pattern Recognition (CVPR), p.1-8. doi: 10.1109/CVPR.2007.383267.

In order to generate a saliency map based on the spectral residual approach, we need to process each channel of an input image separately (single channel in the case of a grayscale input image, and three separate channels in the case of an RGB input image).

The saliency map of a single channel can be generated with the private method `Saliency._get_channel_sal_magn` using the following recipe:

1. Calculate the (magnitude and phase of the) Fourier spectrum of an image, by again using either the `fft` module of NumPy or OpenCV functionality:

```
def _get_channel_sal_magn(self, channel):
    if self.use_numpy_fft:
        img_dft = np.fft.fft2(channel)
        magnitude, angle = cv2.cartToPolar
            (np.real(img_dft), np.imag(img_dft))
    else:
        img_dft = cv2.dft(np.float32(channel),
            flags=cv2.DFT_COMPLEX_OUTPUT)
        magnitude, angle = cv2.cartToPolar
            (img_dft[:, :, 0], img_dft[:, :, 1])
```

2. Calculate the log amplitude of the Fourier spectrum. We will clip the lower bound of magnitudes to 1e-9 in order to prevent a division by zero while calculating the log:

```
log_ampl = np.log10(magnitude.clip(min=1e-9))
```

3. Approximate the averaged spectrum of a typical natural image by convolving the image with a local averaging filter:

```
log_ampl_blur = cv2.blur(log_amlp, (3, 3))
```

4. Calculate the spectral residual. The spectral residual primarily contains the nontrivial (or unexpected) parts of a scene.

```
magn = np.exp(log_amlp - log_ampl_blur)
```

5. Calculate the saliency map by using the inverse Fourier transform, again either via the `fft` module in NumPy or with OpenCV:

```
        if self.use_numpy_fft:
            real_part, imag_part = cv2.polarToCart(residual,
                angle)
```

```
        img_combined = np.fft.ifft2
            (real_part + 1j*imag_part)
        magnitude, _ = cv2.cartToPolar
            ( np.real(img_combined), np.imag(img_combined))
    else:
        img_dft[:, :, 0], img_dft[:, :, 1] =
            cv2.polarToCart(
                residual, angle)
        img_combined = cv2.idft(img_dft)
        magnitude, _ = cv2.cartToPolar
            (img_combined[:, :, 0], img_combined[:, :, 1])
    return magnitude
```

The resulting single-channel saliency map (`magnitude`) is then returned to
`Saliency.get_saliency_map`, where the procedure is repeated for all channels
of the input image. If the input image is grayscale, we are pretty much done:

```
def get_saliency_map(self):
    if self.need_saliency_map:
        # haven't calculated saliency map for this frame yet
        num_channels = 1
        if len(self.frame_orig.shape)==2:
            # single channel
            sal = self._get_channel_sal_magn(self.frame_small)
```

However, if the input image has multiple channels, as is the case for an RGB color
image, we need to consider each channel separately:

```
        else:
            # consider each channel independently
            sal = np.zeros_like
                (self.frame_small).astype(np.float32)
            for c in xrange(self.frame_small.shape[2]):
                sal[:, :, c] = self._get_channel_sal_magn
                    (self.frame_small[:, :, c])
```

The overall salience of a multi-channel image is then determined by the average over
all channels:

```
sal = np.mean(sal, 2)
```

Finally, we need to apply some post-processing, such as an optional blurring stage to
make the result appear smoother:

```
        if self.gauss_kernel is not None:
            sal = cv2.GaussianBlur(sal, self.gauss_kernel,
                sigmaX=8, sigmaY=0)
```

Also, we need to square the values in `sal` in order to highlight the regions of high salience, as outlined by the authors of the original paper. In order to display the image, we scale it back up to its original resolution and normalize the values, so that the largest value is one:

```
sal = sal**2
sal = np.float32(sal)/np.max(sal)
sal = cv2.resize(sal, self.frame_orig.shape[1::-1])
```

In order to avoid having to redo all these intense calculations, we store a local copy of the saliency map for further reference and make sure to lower the flag:

```
self.saliency_map = sal
self.need_saliency_map = False

return self.saliency_map
```

Then, when the user makes subsequent calls to class methods that rely on the calculation of the saliency map under the hood, we can simply refer to the local copy instead of having to do the calculations all over again.

The resulting saliency map then looks like the following image:

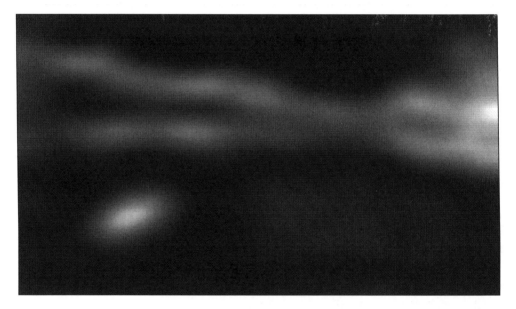

Now we can clearly spot the boat in the water (lower-left corner), which appears as one of the most salient sub-regions of the image. There are other salient regions, too, such as the Grossmünster on the right (have you guessed the city yet?).

By the way, the reason these two areas are the most salient ones in the image seems to be clear and undisputable evidence that the algorithm is aware of the ridiculous number of church towers in the city center of Zurich, effectively prohibiting any chance of them being labeled as "salient".

Detecting proto-objects in a scene

In a sense, the saliency map is already an explicit representation of proto-objects, as it contains only the *interesting* parts of an image. So now that we have done all the hard work, all that is left to do in order to obtain a proto-object map is to threshold the saliency map.

The only open parameter to consider here is the threshold. Setting the threshold too low will result in labeling a lot of regions as proto-objects, including some that might not contain anything of interest (false alarm). On the other hand, setting the threshold too high will ignore most of the salient regions in the image and might leave us with no proto-objects at all. The authors of the original spectral residual paper chose to label only those regions of the image as proto-objects whose saliency was larger than three-times the mean saliency of the image. We give the user the choice to either implement this threshold, or to go with the Otsu threshold by setting the input flag `use_otsu` to `true`:

```
def get_proto_objects_map(self, use_otsu=True):
```

We then retrieve the saliency map of the current frame and make sure to convert it to uint8 precision, so that it can be passed to `cv2.threshold`:

```
saliency = self.get_saliency_map()
if use_otsu:
    _, img_objects = cv2.threshold(np.uint8(saliency*255),
        0, 255, cv2.THRESH_BINARY + cv2.THRESH_OTSU)
```

Otherwise, we will use the threshold `thresh`:

```
else:
    thresh = np.mean(saliency)*255
    _, img_objects = cv2.threshold(np.uint8(saliency*255),
        thresh, 255, cv2.THRESH_BINARY)
return img_objects
```

The resulting proto-objects mask looks like the following image:

The proto-objects mask then serves as an input to the tracking algorithm.

Mean-shift tracking

It turns out that the salience detector discussed previously is already a great tracker of proto-objects by itself. One could simply apply the algorithm to every frame of a video sequence and get a good idea of the location of the objects. However, what is getting lost is correspondence information. Imagine a video sequence of a busy scene, such as from a city center or a sports stadium. Although a saliency map could highlight all the proto-objects in every frame of a recorded video, the algorithm would have no way to know which proto-objects from the previous frame are still visible in the current frame. Also, the proto-objects map might contain some false-positives, such as in the following example:

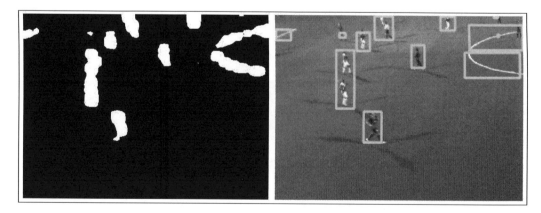

Note that the bounding boxes extracted from the proto-objects map made (at least) three mistakes in the preceding example: it missed highlighting a player (upper-left), merged two players into the same bounding box, and highlighted some additional arguably non-interesting (although visually salient) objects. In order to improve these results, we want to make use of a tracking algorithm.

To solve the correspondence problem, we could use the methods we have learned about previously, such as feature matching and optic flow. Or, we could use a different technique called mean-shift tracking.

Mean-shift is a simple yet very effective technique for tracking arbitrary objects. The intuition behind mean-shift is to consider the pixels in a small region of interest (say, a bounding box of an object we want to track) as sampled from an underlying probability density function that best describes a target.

Consider, for example, the following image:

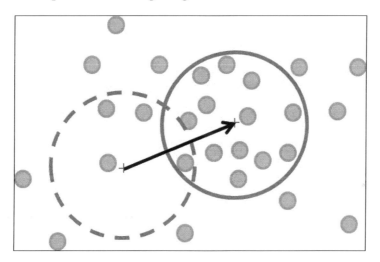

Here, the small gray dots represent samples from a probability distribution. Assume that the closer the dots, the more similar they are to each other. Intuitively speaking, what mean-shift is trying to do is to find the densest region in this landscape and draw a circle around it. The algorithm might start out centering a circle over a region of the landscape that is not dense at all (dashed circle). Over time, it will slowly move towards the densest region (solid circle) and anchor on it. If we design the landscape to be more meaningful than dots (for example, by making the dots correspond to color histograms in the small neighborhoods of an image), we can use mean-shift tracking to find the objects of interest in the scene by finding the histogram that most closely matches the histogram of a target object.

Mean-shift has many applications (such as clustering, or finding the mode of probability density functions), but it is also particularly well-suited to target tracking. In OpenCV, the algorithm is implemented in `cv2.meanShift`, but it requires some pre-processing to function correctly. We can outline the procedure as follows:

1. **Fix a window around each data point**: For example, a bounding box around an object or region of interest.

2. **Compute the mean of data within the window**: In the context of tracking, this is usually implemented as a histogram of the pixel values in the region of interest. For best performance on color images, we will convert to HSV color space.

3. **Shift the window to the mean and repeat until convergence**: This is handled transparently by `cv2.meanShift`. We can control the length and accuracy of the iterative method by specifying termination criteria.

Automatically tracking all players on a soccer field

For the remainder of this chapter, our goal is to combine the saliency detector with mean-shift tracking to automatically track all the players on a soccer field. The proto-objects identified by the salience detector will serve as input to the mean-shift tracker. Specifically, we will focus on a video sequence from the Alfheim dataset, which can be freely obtained from `http://home.ifi.uio.no/paalh/dataset/alfheim/`.

The reason for combining the two algorithms (saliency map and mean-shift tracking), is to remove false positives and improve the accuracy of the overall tracking. This will be achieved in a two-step procedure:

1. Have both the saliency detector and mean-shift tracking assemble a list of bounding boxes for all the proto-objects in a frame. The saliency detector will operate on the current frame, whereas the mean-shift tracker will try to find the proto-objects from the previous frame in the current frame.

2. Keep only those bounding boxes for which both algorithms agree on the location and size. This will get rid of outliers that have been mislabeled as proto-objects by one of the two algorithms.

The hard work is done by the previously introduced `MultiObjectTracker` class and its `advance_frame` method. This method relies on a few private worker methods, which will be explained in detail next. The `advance_frame` method is called whenever a new frame arrives, and accepts a proto-objects map as input:

```
def advance_frame(self, frame, proto_objects_map):
    self.tracker = copy.deepcopy(frame)
```

The method then builds a list of all the candidate bounding boxes, combining the bounding boxes both from the saliency map of the current frame as well as the mean-shift tracking results from the previous to the current frame:

```
# build a list of all bounding boxes
box_all = []

# append to the list all bounding boxes found from the
# current proto-objects map
box_all = self._append_boxes_from_saliency(proto_objects_map,
    box_all)

    # find all bounding boxes extrapolated from last frame
    # via mean-shift tracking
    box_all = self._append_boxes_from_meanshift(frame, box_all)
```

The method then attempts to merge the candidate bounding boxes in order to remove the duplicates. This can be achieved with `cv2.groupRectangles`, which will return a single bounding box if `group_thresh+1` or more bounding boxes overlap in an image:

```
# only keep those that are both salient and in mean shift
if len(self.object_roi)==0:
    group_thresh = 0    # no previous frame: keep all form
    # saliency
else:
    group_thresh = 1 # previous frame + saliency
box_grouped,_ = cv2.groupRectangles(box_all, group_thresh,
    0.1)
```

In order to make mean-shift work, we will have to do some bookkeeping, which will be explained in detail in the following subsections:

```
# update mean-shift bookkeeping for remaining boxes
self._update_mean_shift_bookkeeping(frame, box_grouped)
```

Then we can draw the list of unique bounding boxes on the input image and return the image for plotting:

```
for (x, y, w, h) in box_grouped:
    cv2.rectangle(self.tracker, (x, y), (x + w, y + h),
        (0, 255, 0), 2)

return self.tracker
```

Extracting bounding boxes for proto-objects

The first private worker method is relatively straightforward. It takes a proto-objects map as input as well as a (previously aggregated) list of bounding boxes. To this list, it adds all the bounding boxes found from the contours of the proto-objects:

```
def _append_boxes_from_saliency(self, proto_objects_map, box_all):
    box_sal = []
    cnt_sal, _ = cv2.findContours(proto_objects_map, 1, 2)
```

However, it discards the bounding boxes that are smaller than some threshold, self.min_cnt_area, which is set in the constructor:

```
for cnt in cnt_sal:
    # discard small contours
    if cv2.contourArea(cnt) < self.min_cnt_area:
        continue
```

The result is appended to the box_all list and passed up for further processing:

```
    # otherwise add to list of boxes found from saliency map
    box = cv2.boundingRect(cnt)
    box_all.append(box)

return box_all
```

Setting up the necessary bookkeeping for mean-shift tracking

The second private worker method is concerned with setting up all the bookkeeping that is necessary to perform mean-shift tracking. The method accepts an input image and a list of bounding boxes for which to generate the bookkeeping information:

```
def _update_mean_shift_bookkeeping(self, frame, box_grouped):
```

Bookkeeping mainly consists of calculating a histogram of the HSV color values of each proto-object's bounding box. Thus the input RGB image is converted to HSV right away:

```
hsv = cv2.cvtColor(frame, cv2.COLOR_BGR2HSV)
```

Then, every bounding box in box_grouped is parsed. We need to store both the location and size of the bounding box (self.object_box), as well as a histogram of the HSV color values (self.object_roi):

```
self.object_roi = []
self.object_box = []
```

The location and size of the bounding box is extracted from the list, and the region of interest is cut out of the HSV image:

```
for box in box_grouped:
    (x, y, w, h) = box
    hsv_roi = hsv[y:y + h, x:x + w]
```

We then calculate a histogram of all the hue (H) values in the region of interest. We also ignore the dim or the weakly pronounced areas of the bounding box by using a mask, and normalize the histogram in the end:

```
mask = cv2.inRange(hsv_roi, np.array((0., 60., 32.)),
        np.array((180., 255., 255.)))
roi_hist = cv2.calcHist([hsv_roi], [0], mask, [180], [0, 180])
cv2.normalize(roi_hist, roi_hist, 0, 255, cv2.NORM_MINMAX)
```

We then store this information in the corresponding private member variables, so that it will be available in the very next frame of the process loop, where we will aim to locate the region of interest using the mean-shift algorithm:

```
self.object_roi.append(roi_hist)
self.object_box.append(box)
```

Tracking objects with the mean-shift algorithm

Finally, the third private worker method tracks the proto-objects by using the bookkeeping information stored earlier from the previous frame. Similar to _append_boxes_from_meanshift, we build a list of all the bounding boxes aggregated from mean-shift and pass it up for further processing. The method accepts an input image and a previously aggregated list of bounding boxes:

```
def _append_boxes_from_meanshift(self, frame, box_all):
    hsv = cv2.cvtColor(frame, cv2.COLOR_BGR2HSV)
```

The method then parses all the previously stored proto-objects (from `self.object_roi` and `self.object_box`):

```
for i in xrange(len(self.object_roi)):
    roi_hist = copy.deepcopy(self.object_roi[i])
    box_old = copy.deepcopy(self.object_box[i])
```

In order to find the new, shifted location of a region of interest recorded in the previous image frame, we feed the back-projected region of interest to the mean-shift algorithm. Termination criteria (`self.term_crit`) will make sure to try a sufficient number of iterations (100) and look for mean-shifts of at least some number of pixels (1):

```
dst = cv2.calcBackProject([hsv], [0], roi_hist, [0, 180], 1)
ret, box_new = cv2.meanShift(dst, tuple(box_old),
    self.term_crit)
```

But, before we append the newly detected, shifted bounding box to the list, we want to make sure that we are actually tracking the objects that move. The objects that do not move are most likely false-positives, such as line markings or other visually salient patches that are irrelevant to the task at hand.

In order to discard the irrelevant tracking results, we compare the location of the bounding box from the previous frame (`box_old`) and the corresponding bounding box from the current frame (`box_new`):

```
(xo, yo, wo, ho) = box_old
(xn, yn, wn, hn) = box_new
```

If their centers of mass did not shift at least `sqrt(self.min_shift2)` pixels, we do not include the bounding box in the list:

```
co = [xo + wo/2, yo + ho/2]
cn = [xn + wn/2, yn + hn/2]
if (co[0] - cn[0])**2 + (co[1] - cn[1])**2 >= self.min_shift2:
    box_all.append(box_new)
```

The resulting list of bounding boxes is again passed up for further processing:

```
return box_all
```

Putting it all together

The result of our app can be seen in the following image:

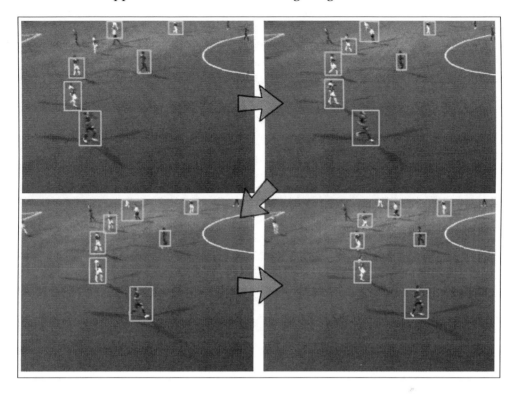

Throughout the video sequence, the algorithm is able to pick up the location of the players, successfully tracking them frame-by-frame by using mean-shift tracking, and combining the resulting bounding boxes with the bounding boxes returned by the salience detector.

It is only through the clever combination of the saliency map and tracking that we can exclude false-positives such as line markings and artifacts of the saliency map. The magic happens in `cv2.groupRectangles`, which requires a similar bounding box to appear at least twice in the `box_all` list, otherwise it is discarded. This means that a bounding box is only then kept in the list if both mean-shift tracking and the saliency map (roughly) agree on the location and size of the bounding box.

Summary

In this chapter, we explored a way to label the potentially *interesting* objects in a visual scene, even if their shape and number is unknown. We explored natural image statistics using Fourier analysis, and implemented a state-of-the-art method for extracting the visually salient regions in the natural scenes. Furthermore, we combined the output of the salience detector with a tracking algorithm to track multiple objects of unknown shape and number in a video sequence of a soccer game.

It would now be possible to extend our algorithm to feature more complicated feature descriptions of proto-objects. In fact, mean-shift tracking might fail when the objects rapidly change size, as would be the case if an object of interest were to come straight at the camera. A more powerful tracker, which comes for free in OpenCV, is `cv2.CamShift`. **CAMShift** stands for Continuously Adaptive Mean-Shift, and bestows upon mean-shift the power to adaptively change the window size. Of course, it would also be possible to simply replace the mean-shift tracker with a previously studied technique such as feature matching or optic flow.

In the next chapter, we will move to the fascinating field of machine learning, which will allow us to build more powerful descriptors of objects. Specifically, we will focus on both detecting (where?) and identifying (what?) the street signs in images. This will allow us to train a classifier that could be used in a dashboard camera in your car, and will familiarize us with the important concepts of machine learning and object recognition.

6
Learning to Recognize Traffic Signs

The goal of this chapter is to train a multiclass classifier to recognize traffic signs. In this chapter, we will cover the following topics:

- Supervised learning concepts
- The **German Traffic Sign Recognition Benchmark (GTSRB)** dataset feature extraction
- **Support vector machines (SVMs)**

We have previously studied how to describe objects by means of keypoints and features, and how to find the correspondence points in two different images of the same physical object. However, our previous approaches were rather limited when it comes to recognizing objects in real-world settings and assigning them to conceptual categories. For example, in *Chapter 2, Hand Gesture Recognition Using a Kinect Depth Sensor*, the required object in the image was a hand, and it had to be nicely placed in the center of the screen. Wouldn't it be nice if we could remove these restrictions?

In this chapter, we will instead train a **Support Vector Machine (SVM)** to recognize all sorts of traffic signs. Although SVMs are binary classifiers (that is, they can be used to learn, at most, two categories: positives and negatives, animals and non-animals, and so on), they can be extended to be used in **multiclass** classification. In order to achieve good classification performance, we will explore a number of color spaces as well as the **Histogram of Oriented Gradients (HOG)** feature. Then, classification performance will be judged based on **accuracy**, **precision**, and **recall**. The following sections will explain all of these terms in detail.

To arrive at such a multiclass classifier, we need to perform the following steps:

1. **Preprocess the dataset**: We need a way to load our dataset, extract the regions of interest, and split the data into appropriate training and test sets.

2. **Extract features**: Chances are that raw pixel values are not the most informative representation of the data. We need a way to extract meaningful features from the data, such as features based on different color spaces and HOG.

3. **Train the classifier**: We will train the multiclass classifier on the training data in two different ways: the **one-vs-all** strategy (where we train a single SVM per class, with the samples of that class as positive samples and all other samples as negatives), and the **one-vs-one** strategy (where we train a single SVM for every pair of classes, with the samples of the first class as positive samples and the samples of the second class as negative samples).

4. **Score the classifier**: We will evaluate the quality of the trained ensemble classifier by calculating different performance metrics, such as accuracy, precision, and recall.

The end result will be an ensemble classifier that achieves a nearly perfect score in classifying 10 different street sign categories:

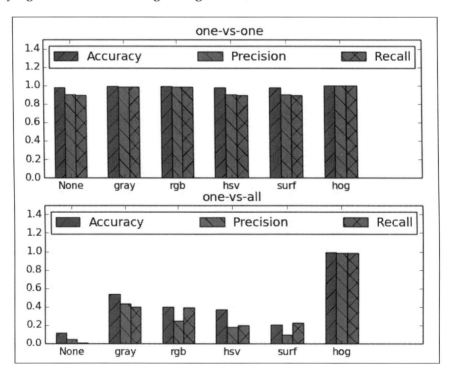

Planning the app

The final app will parse a dataset, train the ensemble classifier, assess its classification performance, and visualize the result. This will require the following components:

- `main`: The main function routine (in `chapter6.py`) for starting the application.

- `datasets.gtsrb`: A script for parsing the German Traffic Sign Recognition Benchmark (GTSRB) dataset. This script contains the following functions:

    ◦ `load_data`: A function used to load the GTSRB dataset, extract a feature of choice, and split the data into training and test sets.

    ◦ `_extract_features`: A function that is called by `load_data` to extract a feature of choice from the dataset.

- `classifiers.Classifier`: An abstract base class that defines the common interface for all classifiers.

- `classifiers.MultiClassSVM`: A class that implements an ensemble of SVMs for multiclass classification using the following public methods:

    ◦ `MultiClassSVM.fit`: A method used to fit the ensemble of SVMs to training data. It takes a matrix of training data as input, where each row is a training sample and the columns contain feature values, and a vector of labels.

    ◦ `MultiClassSVM.evaluate`: A method used to evaluate the ensemble of SVMs by applying it to some test data after training. It takes a matrix of test data as input, where each row is a test sample and the columns contain feature values, and a vector of labels. The function returns three different performance metrics: accuracy, precision, and recall.

In the following sections, we will discuss these steps in detail.

Supervised learning

An important subfield of machine learning is **supervised learning**. In supervised learning, we try to learn from a set of labeled training data; that is, every data sample has a desired target value or true output value. These target values could correspond to the continuous output of a function (such as y in $y = \sin(x)$), or to more abstract and discrete categories (such as *cat* or *dog*). If we are dealing with continuous output, the process is called **regression**, and if we are dealing with discrete output, the process is called **classification**. Predicting housing prices from sizes of houses is an example of regression. Predicting the species from the color of a fish would be classification. In this chapter, we will focus on classification using SVMs.

The training procedure

As an example, we may want to learn what cats and dogs look like. To make this a supervised learning task, we will have to create a database of pictures of both cats and dogs (also called a **training set**), and annotate each picture in the database with its corresponding label: *cat* or *dog*. The task of the program (in literature, it is often referred to as the **learner**) is then to infer the correct label for each of these pictures (that is, for each picture, predict whether it is a picture of a cat or a dog). Based on these predictions, we derive a **score** of how well the learner performed. The score is then used to change the parameters of the learner in order to improve the score over time.

This procedure is outlined in the following figure:

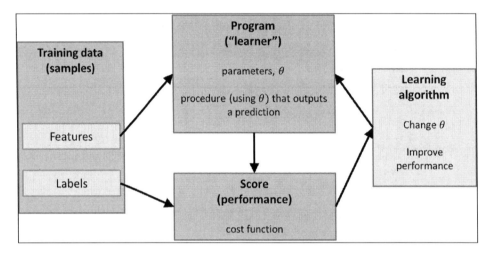

Training data is represented by a set of features. For real-life classification tasks, these features are rarely the raw pixel values of an image, since these tend not to represent the data well. Often, the process of finding the features that best describe the data is an essential part of the entire learning task (also referred to as **feature selection** or **feature engineering**). That is why it is always a good idea to deeply study the statistics and appearances of the training set that you are working with before even thinking about setting up a classifier.

As you are probably aware, there is an entire zoo of learners, cost functions, and learning algorithms out there. These make up the core of the learning procedure. The learner (for example, a linear classifier, support vector machine, or decision tree) defines how input features are converted into a score or cost function (for example, mean-squared error, hinge loss, or entropy), whereas the learning algorithm (for example, gradient descent and backpropagation for neural networks) defines how the parameters of the learner are changed over time.

The training procedure in a classification task can also be thought of as finding an appropriate **decision boundary**, which is a line that best partitions the training set into two subsets, one for each class. For example, consider training samples with only two features (**x** and **y** values) and a corresponding class label (positive, **+**, or negative, **−**). At the beginning of the training procedure, the classifier tries to draw a line to separate all positives from all negatives. As the training progresses, the classifier sees more and more data samples. These are used to update the decision boundary, as illustrated in the following figure:

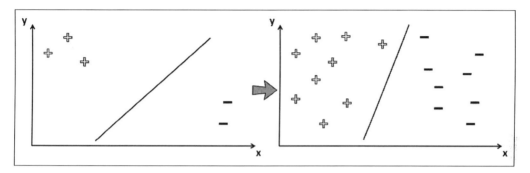

Compared to this simple illustration, an SVM tries to find the optimal decision boundary in a high-dimensional space, so the decision boundary can be more complex than a straight line.

The testing procedure

In order for a trained classifier to be of any practical value, we need to know how it performs when applied to a never-seen-before data sample (also called **generalization**). To stick to our example shown earlier, we want to know which class the classifier predicts when we present it with a previously unseen picture of a cat or a dog.

More generally speaking, we want to know which class the **?** sign in the following figure corresponds to, based on the decision boundary we learned during the training phase:

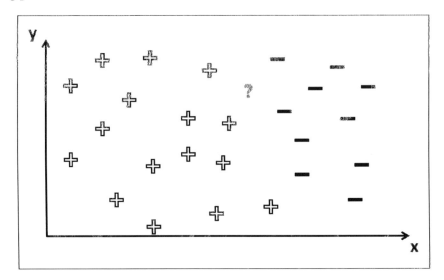

You can see why this is a tricky problem. If the location of the question mark were more to the left, we would be certain that the corresponding class label is **+**. However, in this case, there are several ways to draw the decision boundary such that all the **+** signs are to the left of it and all the **–** signs are to the right of it, as illustrated in this figure:

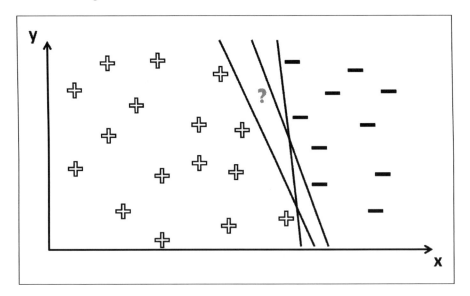

The label of **?** thus depends on the exact decision boundary that was derived during training. If the **?** sign in the preceding figure is actually a **–**, then only one decision boundary (the leftmost) would get the correct answer. A common problem is that training results in a decision boundary that works "too well" on the training set (also known as **overfitting**), but makes a lot of mistakes when applied to unseen data. In that case, it is likely that the learner imprinted details that are specific to the training set on the decision boundary, instead of revealing general properties about the data that might also be true for unseen data.

> A common technique for reducing the effect of overfitting is called **regularization**.

Long story short, the problem always comes back to finding the boundary that best splits, not only the training, but also the test set. That is why the most important metric for a classifier is its generalization performance (that is, how well it classifies data not seen in the training phase).

A classifier base class

From the insights gained in the preceding content, you are now able to write a simple **base class** suitable for all possible classifiers. You can think of this class as a blueprint or recipe that will apply to all classifiers that we are yet to design (we did this with the `BaseLayout` class in *Chapter 1*, *Fun with Filters*). In order to create an **abstract base class (ABC)** in Python, we need to include the `ABCMeta` module:

```
from abc import ABCMeta
```

This allows us to register the class as a `metaclass`:

```
class Classifier:
    """Abstract base class for all classifiers"""
    __metaclass__ = ABCMeta
```

Recall that an abstract class has at least one abstract method. An abstract method is akin to specifying that a certain method must exist, but we are not yet sure what it should look like. We now know that a classifier in its most generic form should contain a method for training, wherein a model is fitted to the training data, and for testing, wherein the trained model is evaluated by applying it to the test data:

```
@abstractmethod
def fit(self, X_train, y_train):
    pass
```

```
@abstractmethod
def evaluate(self, X_test, y_test, visualize=False):
    pass
```

Here, X_train and X_test correspond to the training and test data, respectively, where each row represents a sample, and each column is a feature value of that sample. The training and test labels are passed as y_train and y_test vectors, respectively.

The GTSRB dataset

In order to apply our classifier to traffic sign recognition, we need a suitable dataset. A good choice might be the German Traffic Sign Recognition Benchmark (GTSRB), which contains more than 50,000 images of traffic signs belonging to more than 40 classes. This is a challenging dataset that was used by professionals in a classification challenge during the **International Joint Conference on Neural Networks (IJCNN)** 2011. The dataset can be freely obtained from http://benchmark.ini.rub.de/?section=gtsrb&subsection=dataset.

The GTSRB dataset is perfect for our purposes because it is large, organized, open source, and annotated. However, for the purpose of this book, we will limit the classification to data samples from a total of 10 classes.

Although the actual traffic sign is not necessarily a square, or centered, in each image, the dataset comes with an annotation file that specifies the bounding boxes for each sign.

A good idea before doing any sort of machine learning is usually to get a feeling of the dataset, its qualities, and its challenges. If all the exemplars of the dataset are stored in a list, X, then we can plot a few exemplars with the following script, where we pick a fixed number (sample_size) of random indices (sample_idx) and display each exemplar (X[sample_idx[sp-1]]) in a separate subplot:

```
sample_size = 15
sample_idx = np.random.randint(len(X), size=sample_size)
sp = 1
for r in xrange(3):
    for c in xrange(5):
        ax = plt.subplot(3,5,sp)
        sample = X[sample_idx[sp-1]]
        ax.imshow(sample.reshape((32,32)), cmap=cm.Greys_r)
            ax.axis('off')
        sp += 1
plt.show()
```

The following screenshot shows some examples of this dataset:

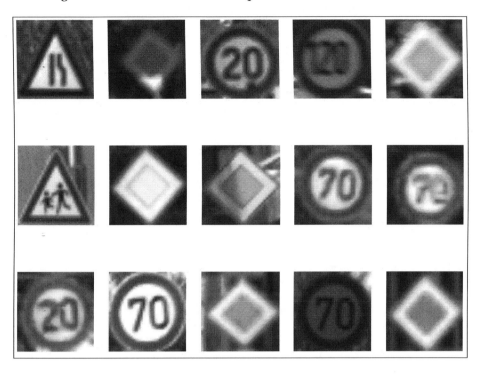

Even from this small data sample, it is immediately clear that this is a challenging dataset for any sort of classifier. The appearances of the signs change drastically based on viewing angle (orientation), viewing distance (blurriness), and lighting conditions (shadows and bright spots). For some of these signs, such as the rightmost sign in the second row, it is difficult even for humans (at least for me) to tell the correct class label right away. Good thing we are aspiring experts of machine learning!

Parsing the dataset

Luckily, the chosen dataset comes with a script for parsing the files (more information can be found at http://benchmark.ini.rub.de/?section=gtsrb&sub section=dataset#Codesnippets).

We spruce it up a bit and adjust it for our purposes. In particular, we want a function that not only loads the dataset, but also extracts a certain feature of interest (via the `feature` input argument), crops the sample to the hand-labeled **Region of Interest (ROI)** containing solely the sample (`cut_roi`), and automatically splits the data into a training and a test set (`test_split`). We also allow the specification of a random seed number (`seed`), and plot some samples for visual inspection (`plot_samples`):

```
import cv2
import numpy as np
import csv

from matplotlib import cm
from matplotlib import pyplot as plt

def load_data(rootpath="datasets", feature="hog", cut_roi=True,
    test_split=0.2, plot_samples=False, seed=113):
```

Although the full dataset contains more than 50,000 examples belonging to 43 classes, for the purpose of this chapter, we will limit ourselves to 10 classes. For easy access, we will hardcode the class labels to use here, but it is straightforward to include more classes (note that you will have to download the entire dataset for this):

```
classes = np.array([0, 4, 8, 12, 16, 20, 24, 28, 32, 36])
```

We then need to iterate over all the classes so as to read all the training samples (to be stored in x) and their corresponding class labels (to be stored in `labels`). Every class has a CSV file containing all of the annotation information for every sample in the class, which we will parse with `csv.reader`:

```
X = [] # images
labels =  []  # corresponding labels

# subdirectory for class
for c in xrange(len(classes)):
    prefix = rootpath + '/' + format(classes[c], '05d') + '/'

    # annotations file
    gt_file = open(prefix + 'GT-'+ format(classes[c], '05d')
        + '.csv')
    gt_reader = csv.reader(gt_file, delimiter=';')
```

Every line of the file contains the annotation for one data sample. We skip the first line (the header) and extract the sample's filename (`row[0]`) so that we can read in the image:

```
gt_reader.next() # skip header
# loop over all images in current annotations file
for row in gt_reader:
    # first column is filename
    im = cv2.imread(prefix + row[0])
```

Occasionally, the object in these samples is not perfectly cut out but is embedded in its surroundings. If the `cut_roi` input argument is set, we will ignore the background and cut out the object using the bounding boxes specified in the annotation file:

```
if cut_roi:
    im = im[np.int(row[4]):np.int(row[6]),
        np.int(row[3]):np.int(row[5]), :]
```

Then, we are ready to append the image (`im`) and its class label (`c`) to our list of samples (`X`) and class labels (`labels`):

```
X.append(im)
labels.append(c)
gt_file.close()
```

Often, it is desirable to perform some form of feature extraction, because raw image data is rarely the best description of the data. We will defer this job to another function, which we will discuss in detail in the next section:

```
if feature is not None:
    X = _extract_feature(X, feature)
```

As pointed out in the previous subsection, it is imperative to keep the samples that we use to train our classifier, separate from the samples that we use to test it. For this, we shuffle the data and split it into two separate sets such that the training set contains a fraction (`1-test_split`) of all samples and the rest of the samples belong to the test set:

```
np.random.seed(seed)
np.random.shuffle(X)
np.random.seed(seed)
np.random.shuffle(labels)

X_train = X[:int(len(X)*(1-test_split))]
y_train = labels[:int(len(X)*(1-test_split))]
X_test = X[int(len(X)*(1-test_split)):]
y_test = labels[int(len(X)*(1-test_split)):]
```

Finally, we can return the extracted data:

```
return (X_train, y_train), (X_test, y_test)
```

Feature extraction

Chances are, that raw pixel values are not the most informative way to represent the data, as we have already realized in *Chapter 3, Finding Objects via Feature Matching and Perspective Transforms*. Instead, we need to derive a measurable property of the data that is more informative for classification.

However, often it is not clear which features would perform best. Instead, it is often necessary to experiment with different features that the modeler finds appropriate. After all, the choice of features might strongly depend on the specific dataset to be analyzed or the specific classification task to be performed. For example, if you have to distinguish between a stop sign and a warning sign, then the most telling feature might be the shape of the sign or the color scheme. However, if you have to distinguish between two warning signs, then color and shape will not help you at all, and you will be required to come up with more sophisticated features.

In order to demonstrate how the choice of features affects classification performance, we will focus on the following:

- A few simple color transformations, such as grayscale, RGB, and HSV. Classification based on grayscale images will give us some baseline performance for the classifier. RGB might give us slightly better performance because of the distinct color schemes of some traffic signs. Even better performance is expected from HSV. This is because it represents colors even more robustly than RGB. Traffic signs tend to have very bright, saturated colors that (ideally) are quite distinct from their surroundings.

- **Speeded-Up Robust Features (SURF)**, which should appear very familiar to you by now. We have previously recognized SURF as an efficient and robust method of extracting meaningful features from an image, so can't we use this technique to our advantage in a classification task?

- **Histogram of Oriented Gradients (HOG)**, which is by far the most advanced feature descriptor to be considered in this chapter. The technique counts occurrences of gradient orientations along a dense grid laid out on the image, and is well-suited for use with SVMs.

Feature extraction is performed by the `gtsrb._extract_features` function, which is implicitly called by `gtsrb.load_data`. It extracts different features as specified by the `feature` input argument.

The easiest case is not to extract any features, instead simply resizing the image to a suitable size:

```
def _extract_feature(X, feature):
    # operate on smaller image
    small_size = (32, 32)
    X = [cv2.resize(x, small_size) for x in X]
```

 For most of the following features, we will be using the (already suitable) default arguments in OpenCV. However, these values are not set in stone, and even in real-world classification tasks, it is often necessary to search across the range of possible values for both feature extracting and learning parameters in a process called **hyperparameter exploration**.

Common preprocessing

There are three common forms of preprocessing that are almost always applied to any data before classification: **mean subtraction**, **normalization**, and **principal component analysis (PCA)**. In this chapter, we will focus on the first two.

Mean subtraction is the most common form of preprocessing (sometimes also referred to as **zero-centering** or **de-meaning**), where the mean value of every feature dimension is calculated across all samples in a dataset. This feature-wise average is then subtracted from every sample in the dataset. You can think of this process as centering the *cloud* of data on the origin. Normalization refers to the scaling of data dimensions so that they are of roughly the same scale. This can be achieved by either dividing each dimension by its standard deviation (once it has been zero-centered), or scaling each dimension to lie in the range of *[-1, 1]*. It makes sense to apply this step only if you have reason to believe that different input features have different scales or units. In the case of images, the relative scales of pixels are already approximately equal (and in the range of *[0, 255]*), so it is not strictly necessary to perform this additional preprocessing step.

In this chapter, the idea is to enhance the local intensity contrast of images so that we do not focus on the overall brightness of an image:

```
# normalize all intensities to be between 0 and 1
X = np.array(X).astype(np.float32) / 255

# subtract mean
X = [x - np.mean(x) for x in X]
```

Grayscale features

The easiest feature to extract is probably the grayscale value of each pixel. Usually, grayscale values are not very indicative of the data they describe, but we will include them here for illustrative purposes (that is, to achieve baseline performance):

```
if feature == 'gray' or feature == 'surf':
    X = [cv2.cvtColor(x, cv2.COLOR_BGR2GRAY) for x in X]
```

Color spaces

Alternatively, you might find that colors contain some information that raw grayscale values cannot capture. Traffic signs often have a distinct color scheme, and it might be indicative of the information it is trying to convey (that is, red for stop signs and forbidden actions, green for informational signs, and so on). We could opt for using the RGB images as input, in which case we do not have to do anything, since the dataset is already RGB.

However, even RGB might not be informative enough. For example, a stop sign in broad daylight might appear very bright and clear, but its colors might appear much less vibrant on a rainy or foggy day. A better choice might be the HSV color space, which rearranges RGB color values in a cylindrical coordinate space along the axes of **hue**, **saturation**, and **value** (or brightness). The most telling feature of traffic signs in this color space might be the hue (a more perceptually relevant description of color or chromaticity), better distinguishing the color scheme of different sign types. Saturation and value could be equally important, however, as traffic signs tend to use relatively bright and saturated colors that do not typically appear in natural scenes (that is, their surroundings).

In OpenCV, the HSV color space is only a single call to cv2.cvtColor away:

```
if feature == 'hsv':
    X = [cv2.cvtColor(x, cv2.COLOR_BGR2HSV) for x in X]
```

Speeded Up Robust Features

But wait a minute! In *Chapter 3, Finding Objects via Feature Matching and Perspective Transforms* you learned that the SURF descriptor is one of the best and most robust ways to describe images independent of scale or rotations. Can we use this technique to our advantage in a classification task?

Glad you asked! To make this work, we need to adjust SURF so that it returns a fixed number of features per image. By default, the SURF descriptor is only applied to a small list of *interesting* keypoints in the image, the number of which might differ on an image-by-image basis. This is unsuitable for our current purposes, because we want to find a fixed number of feature values per data sample.

Instead, we need to apply SURF to a fixed dense grid laid out over the image, which can be achieved by creating a *dense* feature detector:

```
if feature == 'surf':
    # create dense grid of keypoints
    dense = cv2.FeatureDetector_create("Dense")
    kp = dense.detect(np.zeros(small_size).astype(np.uint8))
```

Then it is possible to obtain SURF descriptors for each point on the grid and append that data sample to our feature matrix. We initialize SURF with a `minHessian` value of 400 as we did before, and:

```
surf = cv2.SURF(400)
surf.upright = True
surf.extended = True
```

Keypoints and descriptors can then be obtained via this code:

```
kp_des = [surf.compute(x, kp) for x in X]
```

Because `surf.compute` has two output arguments, `kp_des` will actually be a concatenation of both keypoints and descriptors. The second element in the `kp_des` array is the descriptor that we care about. We select the first `num_surf_features` from each data sample and add it back to the training set:

```
num_surf_features = 36
X = [d[1][:num_surf_features, :] for d in kp_des]
```

Histogram of Oriented Gradients

The last feature descriptor to consider is the Histogram of Oriented Gradients (HOG). HOG features have previously been shown to work exceptionally well in combination with SVMs, especially when applied to tasks such as pedestrian recognition.

The essential idea behind HOG features is that the local shapes and appearance of objects within an image can be described by the distribution of edge directions. The image is divided into small connected regions, within which a histogram of gradient directions (or edge directions) is compiled. Then, the descriptor is assembled by concatenating the different histograms. For improved performance, the local histograms can be contrast-normalized, which results in better invariance to changes in illumination and shadowing. You can see why this sort of preprocessing might just be the perfect fit for recognizing traffic signs under different viewing angles and lighting conditions.

The HOG descriptor is fairly accessible in OpenCV by means of `cv2.HOGDescriptor`, which takes the detection window size (32 x 32), the block size (16 x 16), the cell size (8 x 8), and the cell stride (8 x 8), as input arguments. For each of these cells, the HOG descriptor then calculates a histogram of oriented gradients using nine bins:

```
elif feature == 'hog':
    # histogram of oriented gradients
    block_size = (small_size[0] / 2, small_size[1] / 2)
    block_stride = (small_size[0] / 4, small_size[1] / 4)
    cell_size = block_stride
    num_bins = 9
    hog = cv2.HOGDescriptor(small_size, block_size,
        block_stride, cell_size, num_bins)
```

Applying the HOG descriptor to every data sample is then as easy as calling `hog.compute`:

```
X = [hog.compute(x) for x in X]
```

After we have extracted all the features we want, we should remember to have `gtsrb._extract_features` return the assembled list of data samples so that they can be split into training and test sets:

```
X = [x.flatten() for x in X]
return X
```

Now, we are finally ready to train the classifier on the preprocessed dataset.

Support Vector Machine

A Support Vector Machine (SVM) is a learner for binary classification (and regression) that tries to separate examples from the two different class labels with a decision boundary that maximizes the margin between the two classes.

Let's return to our example of positive and negative data samples, each of which has exactly two features (**x** and **y**) and two possible decision boundaries, as follows:

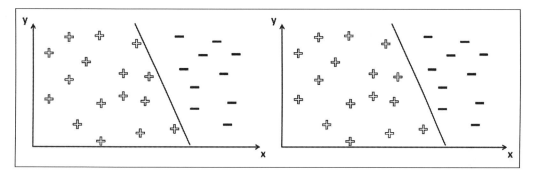

Both of these decision boundaries get the job done. They partition all the samples of positives and negatives with zero misclassifications. However, one of them seems intuitively better. How can we quantify "better" and thus learn the "best" parameter settings?

This is where SVMs come in. SVMs are also called maximal margin classifiers because they can be used to do exactly that; they define the decision boundary so as to make those two clouds of + and − as far apart as possible.

For the preceding example, an SVM would find two lines that pass through the data points on the class margins (the dashed lines in the following figure), and then make the line that passes through the center of the margins, the decision boundary (the bold black line in the following figure):

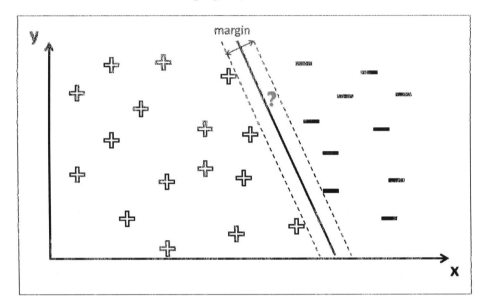

It turns out that to find the maximal margin, it is only important to consider the data points that lie on the class margins. These points are sometimes also called **support vectors**.

 In addition to performing linear classification (that is, when the decision boundary is a straight line), SVMs can also perform a non-linear classification using what is called the **kernel trick**, implicitly mapping their inputs to high-dimensional feature spaces.

Using SVMs for Multi-class classification

Whereas some classification algorithms, such as neural networks, naturally lend themselves to using more than two classes, SVMs are binary classifiers by nature. They can, however, be turned into multiclass classifiers.

Here, we will consider two different strategies:

- **one-vs-all**: The one-vs-all strategy involves training a single classifier per class, with the samples of that class as positive samples and all other samples as negatives. For k classes, this strategy thus requires the training of k different SVMs. During testing, all classifiers can express a "+1" vote by predicting that an unseen sample belongs to their class. In the end, an unseen sample is classified by the ensemble as the class with the most votes. Usually, this strategy is used in combination with confidence scores instead of predicted labels so that in the end, the class with the highest confidence score can be picked.

- **one-vs-one**: The one-vs-one strategy involves training a single classifier per class pair, with the samples of the first class as positive samples and the samples of the second class as negative samples. For k classes, this strategy requires the training of k*(k-1)/2 classifiers. However, the classifiers have to solve a significantly easier task, so there is a trade-off when considering which strategy to use. During testing, all classifiers can express a "+1" vote for either the first or the second class. In the end, an unseen sample is classified by the ensemble as the class with the most votes.

Which strategy to use can be specified by the user via an input argument (mode) to the MutliClassSVM class:

```
class MultiClassSVM(Classifier):
    """Multi-class classification using Support Vector Machines
        (SVMs) """
    def __init__(self, num_classes, mode="one-vs-all",
        params=None):
        self.num_classes = num_classes
        self.mode = mode
        self.params = params or dict()
```

As mentioned earlier, depending on the classification strategy, we will need either k or k*(k-1)/2 SVM classifiers, for which we will maintain a list in self.classifiers:

```
# initialize correct number of classifiers
self.classifiers = []
if mode == "one-vs-one":
    # k classes: need k*(k-1)/2 classifiers
    for i in xrange(numClasses*(numClasses-1)/2):
        self.classifiers.append(cv2.SVM())
elif mode == "one-vs-all":
```

```
                # k classes: need k classifiers
                for i in xrange(numClasses):
                        self.classifiers.append(cv2.SVM())
            else:
                    print "Unknown mode ",mode
```

Once the classifiers are correctly initialized, we are ready for training.

Training the SVM

Following the requirements defined by the `Classifier` base class, we need to perform training in a `fit` method:

```
def fit(self, X_train, y_train, params=None):
    """ fit model to data """
    if params is None:
        params = self.params
```

The training will differ depending on the classification strategy that is being used. The one-vs-one strategy requires us to train an SVM for each pair of classes:

```
if self.mode == "one-vs-one":
    svm_id=0
    for c1 in xrange(self.numClasses):
        for c2 in xrange(c1+1,self.numClasses):
```

Here we use `svm_id` to keep track of the number of SVMs we use. In contrast to the one-vs-all strategy, we need to train a much larger number of SVMs here. However, the training samples to consider per SVM include only samples of either class—c1 or c2:

```
y_train_c1 = np.where(y_train==c1)[0]
y_train_c2 = np.where(y_train==c2)[0]

data_id = np.sort(np.concatenate((y_train_c1,
    y_train_c2), axis=0))
X_train_id = X_train[data_id,:]
y_train_id = y_train[data_id]
```

Because an SVM is a binary classifier, we need to convert our integer class labels into 0s and 1s. We assign label 1 to all samples of the c1 class, and label 0 to all samples of the c2 class, again using the handy `np.where` function:

```
y_train_bin = np.where(y_train_id==c1, 1,
    0).flatten()
```

Then we are ready to train the SVM:

```
self.classifiers[svm_id].train(X_train_id,
    y_train_bin, params=self.params)
```

Here, we pass a dictionary of training parameters, `self.params`, to the SVM. For now, we only consider the (already suitable) default parameter values, but feel free to experiment with different settings.

Don't forget to update `svm_id` so that you can move on to the next SVM in the list:

```
svm_id += 1
```

On the other hand, the one-vs-all strategy requires us to train a total of `self.numClasses` SVMs, which makes indexing a lot easier:

```
elif self.mode == "one-vs-all":
    for c in xrange(self.numClasses):
```

Again, we need to convert integer labels to binary labels. In contrast to the one-vs-one strategy, every SVM here considers all training samples. We assign label 1 to all samples of the c class and label 0 to all other samples, and pass the data to the classifier's training method:

```
y_train_bin = np.where(y_train==c,1,0).flatten()
self.classifiers[c].train(X_train, y_train_bin,
    params=self.params)
```

OpenCV will take care of the rest. What happens under the hood is that the SVM training uses Lagrange multipliers to optimize some constraints that lead to the maximum-margin decision boundary. The optimization process is usually performed until some termination criteria are met, which can be specified via the SVM's optional arguments:

```
params.term_crit = (cv2.TERM_CRITERIA_EPS +
    cv2.TERM_CRITERIA_MAX_ITER, 100, 1e-6)
```

Testing the SVM

There are many ways to evaluate a classifier, but most often, we are simply interested in the accuracy metric, that is, how many data samples from the test set were classified correctly.

In order to arrive at this metric, we need to have each individual SVM predict the labels of the test data, and assemble their consensus in a 2D voting matrix (Y_vote):

```
def evaluate(self, X_test, y_test, visualize=False):
    """Evaluates model performance"""
    Y_vote = np.zeros((len(y_test), self.numClasses))
```

For each sample in the dataset, the voting matrix will contain the number of times the sample has been voted to belong to a certain class. Populating the voting matrix will take a slightly different form depending on the classification strategy. In the case of the one-vs-one strategy, we need to loop over all k*(k-1)/2 classifiers and obtain a vector, called y_hat, that contains the predicted labels for all test samples that belong to either the c1 class or the c2 class:

```
if self.mode == "one-vs-one":
    svm_id = 0
    for c1 in xrange(self.numClasses):
        for c2 in xrange(c1+ 1, self.numClasses):
            data_id = np.where((y_test==c1) + (y_test==c2))[0]
            X_test_id = X_test[data_id, :],:],:]
            y_test_id = y_test[data_id]

            # predict labels
            y_hat = self.classifiers[svm_id].predict_all
                ( X_test_id)
```

The y_hat vector will contain 1s whenever the classifier believes that the sample belongs to the c1 class, and 0s wherever the classifier believes that the sample belongs to the c2 class. The tricky part is how to +1 the correct cell in the Y_vote matrix. For example, if the *ith* entry in y_hat is 1 (meaning that we believe that the *ith* sample belongs to the c1 class), we want to increment the value of the *ith* row and *c1th* column in the Y_vote matrix. This will indicate that the present classifier expressed a vote to classify the *ith* sample as belonging to the c1 class.

Since we know the indices of all test samples that belong to either class, c1 or c2 (stored in data_id), we know which rows of Y_vote to access. Because data_id is used as an index for Y_vote, we only need to find the indices in data_id that correspond to entries where y_hat is 1:

```
# we vote for c1 where y_hat is 1, and for c2 where
# y_hat is 0
# np.where serves as the inner index into the
# data_id array, which in turn serves as index
# into the Y_vote matrix
Y_vote[data_id[np.where(y_hat==1)[0]],c1] += 1
```

Similarly, we can express a vote for the c2 class:

```
Y_vote[data_id[np.where(y_hat==0)[0]],c2] += 1
```

Then we increment svm_id and move on to the next classifier:

```
svm_id += 1
```

The one-vs-all strategy poses a different problem. Indexing in the Y_vote matrix is less tricky, because we always consider all the test data samples. We repeat the procedure of predicting labels for each data sample:

```
elif self.mode == "one-vs-all":
    for c in xrange(self.numClasses):
        # predict labels
        y_hat = self.classifiers[c].predict_all(X_test)
```

Wherever y_hat has a value of 1, the classifier expresses a vote that the data sample belongs to class c, and we update the voting matrix:

```
# we vote for c where y_hat is 1
if np.any(y_hat):
    Y_vote[np.where(y_hat==1)[0], c] += 1
```

The tricky part now is, "What to do with entries of y_hat that have a value of 0?" Since we classified one-vs-all, we only know that the sample is not of the c class (that is, it belongs to the "rest"), but we do not know what the exact class label is supposed to be. Thus, we cannot add these samples to the voting matrix.

Since we neglected to include samples that are consistently classified as belonging to the "rest," it is possible that some rows in the Y_vote matrix will have all 0s. In such a case, simply pick a class at random (unless you have a better idea):

```
# find all rows without votes, pick a class at random
no_label = np.where(np.sum(y_vote,axis=1)==0)[0]
Y_vote[no_label,np.random.randint(self.numClasses,
    size=len(no_label))] = 1
```

Now, we are ready to calculate the desired performance metrics as described in detail in later sections. For the purpose of this chapter, we choose to calculate accuracy, precision, and recall, which are implemented in their own dedicated private methods:

```
accuracy = self.__accuracy(y_test, Y_vote)
precision = self.__precision(y_test, Y_vote)
recall = self.__recall(y_test, Y_vote)

return (accuracy,precision,recall)
```

The scikit-learn machine learning package (http://scikit-learn.org) supports the three metrics — accuracy, precision, and recall (as well as others) — straight out of the box, and also comes with a variety of other useful tools. For educational purposes (and to minimize software dependencies), we will derive the three metrics ourselves.

Confusion matrix

A confusion matrix is a 2D matrix of size equal to (self.numClasses, self.numClasses), where the rows correspond to the predicted class labels, and columns correspond to the actual class labels. Then, the [r,c] matrix element contains the number of samples that were predicted to have label r, but in reality have label c. Having access to a confusion matrix will allow us to calculate precision and recall.

The confusion matrix can be calculated from a vector of ground-truth labels (y_test) and the voting matrix (Y_vote). We first convert the voting matrix into a vector of predicted labels by picking the column index (that is, the class label) that received the most votes:

```
def __confusion(self, y_test, Y_vote):
    y_hat = np.argmax(Y_vote, axis=1)
```

Then we need to loop twice over all classes and count the number of times a data sample of the c_true ground-truth class was predicted as having the c_pred class:

```
conf = np.zeros((self.numClasses,
    self.numClasses)).astype(np.int32)
for c_true in xrange(self.numClasses):
    # looking at all samples of a given class, c_true
    # how many were classified as c_true? how many as others?
    for c_pred in xrange(self.numClasses):
```

All elements of interest in each iteration are thus the samples that have the c_true label in y_test and the c_pred label in y_hat:

```
y_this = np.where((y_test==c_true) * (y_hat==c_pred))
```

The corresponding cell in the confidence matrix is then the number of non-zero elements in y_this:

```
conf[c_pred,c_true] = np.count_nonzero(y_this)
```

After the nested loops complete, we pass the confusion matrix for further processing:

```
return conf
```

As you may have guessed already, the goal of a good classifier is to make the confusion matrix diagonal, which would imply that the ground-truth class (c_true) and the predicted class (c_pred) of every sample are the same.

The one-vs-one strategy, in combination with HOG features, actually performs really well, which is evident from this resulting confusion matrix, wherein most of the off-diagonal elements are zero:

```
[[ 52    0    0    0    0    1    0    0    0    0]
 [  0  387    1    1    0    1    0    0    0    0]
 [  0    2  288    0    0    1    0    0    0    0]
 [  0    0    0  419    0    0    0    0    1    0]
 [  0    0    1    0   69    1    0    0    0    0]
 [  0    0    0    0    0   76    0    1    0    0]
 [  0    0    0    0    0    0   49    0    0    0]
 [  0    0    0    0    0    0    1  116    0    0]
 [  1    0    0    0    0    0    0    1   46    0]
 [  0    0    0    1    0    1    0    0    0   65]]
```

Accuracy

The most straightforward metric to calculate is probably accuracy. This metric simply counts the number of test samples that have been predicted correctly, and returns the number as a fraction of the total number of test samples:

```
def __accuracy(self, y_test, y_vote):
    """ Calculates the accuracy based on a vector of ground-truth
        labels (y_test) and a 2D voting matrix (y_vote) of size
        (len(y_test),numClasses). """
```

The classification prediction (y_hat) can be extracted from the vote matrix by finding out which class has received the most votes:

```
y_hat = np.argmax(y_vote, axis=1)
```

The correctness of the prediction can be verified by comparing the predicted label of a sample to its actual label:

```
# all cases where predicted class was correct
mask = (y_hat == y_test)
```

Accuracy is then calculated by counting the number of correct predictions (that is, non-zero entries in `mask`) and normalizing that number by the total number of test samples:

```
return np.count_nonzero(mask)*1./len(y_test)
```

Precision

Precision in binary classification is a useful metric for measuring the fraction of retrieved instances that are relevant (also called the **positive predictive value**). In a classification task, the number of **true positives** is defined as the number of items correctly labeled as belonging to the positive class. **Precision** is defined as the number of true positives divided by the total number of positives. In other words, out of all the pictures in the test set that a classifier thinks contain a cat, precision is the fraction of pictures that actually contain a cat.

The total number of positives can also be calculated as the sum of true positives and **false positives**, the latter being the number of samples incorrectly labeled as belonging to a particular class. This is where the confusion matrix comes in handy, because it will allow us to quickly calculate the number of false positives.

Again, we start by translating the voting matrix into a vector of predicted labels:

```
def __precision(self, y_test, Y_vote):
    """ precision extended to multi-class classification """
    # predicted classes
    y_hat = np.argmax(Y_vote, axis=1)
```

The procedure will differ slightly depending on the classification strategy. The one-vs-one strategy requires us operating with the confusion matrix:

```
if True or self.mode == "one-vs-one":
    # need confusion matrix
    conf = self.__confusion(y_test, y_vote)

    # consider each class separately
    prec = np.zeros(self.numClasses)
    for c in xrange(self.numClasses):
```

Since true positives are the samples that are predicted to have label c and also have label c in reality, they correspond to the diagonal elements of the confusion matrix:

```
# true positives: label is c, classifier predicted c
tp = conf[c,c]
```

Similarly, false positives correspond to the off-diagonal elements of the confusion matrix that are in the same column as the true positive. The quickest way to calculate that number is to sum up all the elements in column c but subtract the true positives:

```
# false positives: label is c, classifier predicted
# not c
fp = np.sum(conf[:,c]) - conf[c,c]
```

Precision is the number of true positives divided by the sum of true positives and false positives:

```
if tp + fp != 0:
    prec[c] = tp*1./(tp+fp)
```

The one-vs-all strategy makes the math slightly easier. Since we always operate on the full test set, we need to find only those samples that have a ground-truth label of c in y_test and a predicted label of c in y_hat:

```
elif self.mode == "one-vs-all":
    # consider each class separately
    prec = np.zeros(self.numClasses)
    for c in xrange(self.numClasses):
        # true positives: label is c, classifier predicted c
        tp = np.count_nonzero((y_test==c) * (y_hat==c))
```

Similarly, false positives have a ground-truth label of c in y_test and their predicted label is not c in y_hat:

```
# false positives: label is c, classifier predicted
# not c
fp = np.count_nonzero((y_test==c) * (y_hat!=c))
```

Again, precision is the number of true positives divided by the sum of true positives and false positives:

```
if tp + fp != 0:
    prec[c] = tp*1./(tp+fp)
```

After that, we pass the precision vector for visualization:

```
return prec
```

Recall

Recall is similar to precision in the sense that it measures the fraction of relevant instances that are retrieved (as opposed to the fraction of retrieved instances that are relevant). In a classification task, the number of false negatives is the number of items not labeled as belonging to the positive class but should have been labeled. Recall is the number of true positives divided by the sum of true positives and false negatives. In other words, out of all the pictures of cats in the world, recall is the fraction of pictures that have been correctly identified as pictures of cats.

Again, we start off by translating the voting matrix into a vector of predicted labels:

```
def __recall(self, y_test, Y_vote):
    """ recall extended to multi-class classification """
    # predicted classes
    y_hat = np.argmax(Y_vote, axis=1)
```

The procedure is almost identical to calculating precision. The one-vs-one strategy once again requires some arithmetic involving the confusion matrix:

```
if True or self.mode == "one-vs-one":
    # need confusion matrix
    conf = self.__confusion(y_test, y_vote)

    # consider each class separately
    recall = np.zeros(self.numClasses)
    for c in xrange(self.numClasses):
```

True positives once again correspond to diagonal elements in the confusion matrix:

```
        # true positives: label is c, classifier predicted c
        tp = conf[c,c]
```

To get the number of false negatives, we sum up all the columns in the row c and subtract the number of true positives for this row. This will give us the number of samples for which the classifier predicted the class as c but that actually had a ground-truth label other than c:

```
        # false negatives: label is not c, classifier
        # predicted c
        fn = np.sum(conf[c,:]) - conf[c,c]
```

Recall is the number of true positives divided by the sum of true positives and false negatives:

```
        if tp + fn != 0:
            recall[c] = tp*1./(tp+fn)
```

Again, the one-vs-all strategy makes the math slightly easier. Since we always operate on the full test set, we need to find only those samples whose ground-truth label is not c in y_test, and predicted label is c in y_hat:

```
elif self.mode == "one-vs-all":
    # consider each class separately
    recall = np.zeros(self.numClasses)
    for c in xrange(self.numClasses):
        # true positives: label is c, classifier predicted c
        tp = np.count_nonzero((y_test==c) * (y_hat==c))

        # false negatives: label is not c, classifier
        # predicted c
        fn = np.count_nonzero((y_test!=c) * (y_hat==c))

        if tp + fn != 0:
            recall[c] = tp*1./(tp+fn)
```

After that, we pass the recall vector for visualization:

```
return recall
```

Putting it all together

To run our app, we will need to execute the main function routine (in chapter6.py). It loads the data, trains the classifier, evaluates its performance, and visualizes the result.

But first, we need to import all the relevant modules and set up a main function:

```
import numpy as np

import matplotlib.pyplot as plt
from datasets import gtsrb
from classifiers import MultiClassSVM


def main():
```

Then, the goal is to compare classification performance across settings and feature extraction methods. This includes running the task with both classification strategies, one-vs-all and one-vs-one, as well as preprocessing the data with a list of different feature extraction approaches:

```
strategies = ['one-vs-one', 'one-vs-all']features = [None,
    'gray', 'rgb', 'hsv', 'surf', 'hog']
```

For each of these settings, we need to collect three performance metrics—accuracy, precision, and recall:

```
accuracy = np.zeros((2,len(features)))
precision = np.zeros((2,len(features)))
recall = np.zeros((2,len(features)))
```

A nested `for` loop will run the classifier with all of these settings and populate the performance metric matrices. The outer loop is over all elements in the `features` vector:

```
for f in xrange(len(features)):
    (X_train,y_train), (X_test,y_test) = gtsrb.load_data(
        "datasets/gtsrb_training",
        feature=features[f], test_split=0.2)
```

Before passing the training data (`X_train,y_train`) and test data (`X_test,y_test`) to the classifiers, we want to make sure that they are in the format that the classifier expects; that is, each data sample is stored in a row of `X_train` or `X_test`, with the columns corresponding to feature values:

```
X_train = np.squeeze(np.array(X_train)).astype(np.float32)
y_train = np.array(y_train)
X_test = np.squeeze(np.array(X_test)).astype(np.float32)
y_test = np.array(y_test)
```

We also need to know the number of class labels (since we did not load the complete GTSRB dataset). This can be achieved by concatenating `y_train` and `y_test` and extracting all unique labels in the combined list:

```
labels = np.unique(np.hstack((y_train,y_test)))
```

Next, the inner loop iterates over all the elements in the `strategies` vector, which currently includes the two strategies, one-vs-all and one-vs-one:

```
for s in xrange(len(strategies)):
```

Then we instantiate the `MultiClassSVM` class with the correct number of unique labels and the corresponding classification strategy:

```
MCS = MultiClassSVM(len(labels),strategies[s])
```

Now we are all ready to apply the ensemble classifier to the training data and extract the three performance metrics after training:

```
MCS.fit(X_train, y_train)
(accuracy[s,f],precision[s,f],recall[s,f]) =
    MCS.evaluate(X_test, y_test)
```

This ends the nested `for` loop. All that is left to do is to visualize the result. For this, we choose matplotlib's bar plot functionality. The goal is to show the three performance metrics (accuracy, precision, and recall) for all combinations of extracted features and classification strategies. We will use one plotting window per classification strategy, and arrange the corresponding data in a stacked bar plot:

```
f,ax = plt.subplots(2)
for s in xrange(len(strategies)):
    x = np.arange(len(features))
    ax[s].bar(x-0.2, accuracy[s,:], width=0.2, color='b',
        hatch='/', align='center')
    ax[s].bar(x, precision[s,:], width=0.2, color='r',
        hatch='\\', align='center')
    ax[s].bar(x+0.2, recall[s,:], width=0.2, color='g',
        hatch='x', align='center')
```

For the sake of visibility, the y axis is restricted to the relevant range:

```
ax[s].axis([-0.5, len(features) + 0.5, 0, 1.5])
```

Finally, we add some plot decorations:

```
ax[s].legend(('Accuracy','Precision','Recall'), loc=2,
    ncol=3, mode="expand")
ax[s].set_xticks(np.arange(len(features)))
ax[s].set_xticklabels(features)
ax[s].set_title(strategies[s])
```

Now the data is ready to be plotted!

```
plt.show()
```

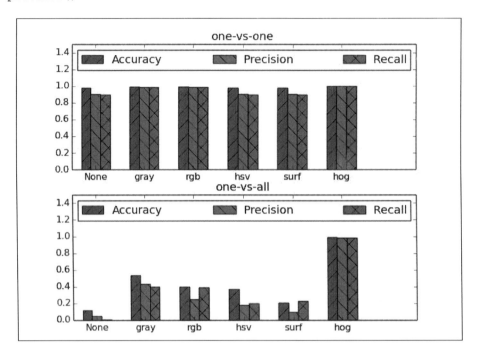

This screenshot contains a lot of information, so let's break it down step by step:

- The most straightforward observation is that the HOG feature seems mighty powerful! This feature has outperformed all other features, no matter what the classification strategy is. Again, this highlights the importance of feature extraction, which generally requires a deep understanding of the statistics of the dataset under study.

- Interestingly, with the use of the one-vs-one strategy, all approaches led to an accuracy north of 0.95, which might stem from the fact that a binary classification task (with two possible class labels) is sometimes easier to learn than a 10-class classification task. Unfortunately, the same cannot be said for the one-vs-all approach. But to be fair, the one-vs-all approach had to operate with only 10 SVMs, whereas the one-vs-one approach had 45 SVMs to work with. This gap is only likely to increase if we add more object categories.

- The effect of de-meaning can be seen by comparing the result for None with the result for rgb. These two settings were identical, except that the samples under rgb were normalized. The difference in performance is evident, especially for the one-vs-all strategy.

- A little disappointing is the finding that none of the color transformations (neither RGB nor HSV) were able to perform significantly better than the simple grayscale transform. SURF did not help either.

Summary

In this chapter, we trained a multiclass classifier to recognize traffic signs from the GTSRB database. We discussed the basics of supervised learning, explored the intricacies of feature extraction, and extended SVMs so that they can be used for multiclass classification.

Notably, we left out some details along the way, such as attempting to fine-tune the hyperparameters of the learning algorithm. When we restrict the traffic sign dataset to only 10 classes, the default values of the various function arguments along the way, seem to be sufficient for performing exceptionally well (just look at the perfect score achieved with the HOG feature and the one-vs-one strategy). With this functional setup and a good understanding of the underlying methodology, you can now try to classify the entire GTSRB dataset! It is definitely worth taking a look at their website, where you will find classification results for a variety of classifiers. Maybe, your own approach will soon be added to the list.

In the next (and last) chapter, we will move even deeper into the field of machine learning. Specifically, we will focus on recognizing emotional expressions in human faces using convolutional neural networks. This time, we will combine the classifier with a framework for object detection, which will allow us to localize (where?) a human face in an image, and then focus on identifying (what?) the emotional expression contained in that face. This will conclude our quest into the depths of machine learning, and provide you with all the necessary tools to develop your own advanced OpenCV projects using the principles and concepts of computer vision.

7
Learning to Recognize Emotions on Faces

We previously familiarized ourselves with the concepts of object detection and object recognition, but we never combined them to develop an app that can do both end-to-end. For the final chapter in this book, we will do exactly that.

The goal of this chapter is to develop an app that combines both **face detection** and **face recognition**, with a focus on recognizing emotional expressions in the detected face.

For this, we will touch upon two other classic algorithms that come bundled with OpenCV: **Haar Cascade Classifiers** and **multi-layer peceptrons** (**MLPs**). While the former can be used to rapidly detect (or locate, answering the question: where?) objects of various sizes and orientations in an image, the latter can be used to recognize them (or identify, answering the question: what?).

The end goal of the app will be to detect your own face in each captured frame of a webcam live stream and label your emotional expression. To make this task feasible, we will limit ourselves to the following possible emotional expressions: neutral, happy, sad, surprised, angry, and disgusted.

To arrive at such an app, we need to solve the following two challenges:

- **Face detection**: We will use the popular Haar cascade classifier by Viola and Jones, for which OpenCV provides a whole range of pre-trained exemplars. We will make use of face cascades and eye cascades to reliably detect and align facial regions from frame to frame.

- **Facial expression recognition**: We will train a multi-layer perceptron to recognize the six different emotional expressions listed earlier, in every detected face. The success of this approach will crucially depend on the training set that we assemble, and the preprocessing that we choose to apply to each sample in the set. In order to improve the quality of our self-recorded training set, we will make sure that all data samples are aligned using **affine transformations** and reduce the dimensionality of the feature space by applying **Principal Component Analysis (PCA)**. The resulting representation is sometimes also referred to as **Eigenfaces**.

The reliable recognition of faces and facial expressions is a challenging task for artificial intelligence, yet humans are able to perform these kinds of tasks with apparent ease. Today's state-of-the-art models range all the way from 3D deformable face models fitting over convolutional neural networks, to deep learning algorithms. Granted, these approaches are significantly more sophisticated than our approach. Yet, MLPs are classic algorithms that helped transform the field of machine learning, so for educational purposes, we will stick to a set of algorithms that come bundled with OpenCV.

We will combine the algorithms mentioned earlier in a single end-to-end app that annotates a detected face with the corresponding facial expression label in each captured frame of a video live stream. The end result might look something like the following image, capturing my reaction when the code first compiled:

Planning the app

The final app will consist of a main script that integrates the process flow end-to-end, from face detection to facial expression recognition, as well as some utility functions to help along the way.

Thus, the end product will require several components:

- `chapter7`: The main script and entry-point for the chapter.
- `chapter7.FaceLayout`: A custom layout based on `gui.BaseLayout` that operates in two different modes:
    - Training mode: In the training mode, the app will collect image frames, detect a face therein, assign a label depending on the facial expression, and upon exiting, save all the collected data samples in a file, so that it can be parsed by `datasets.homebrew`.
    - Testing mode: In the testing mode, the app will detect a face in each video frame and predict the corresponding class label by using a pre-trained MLP.
- `chapter3.main`: The main function routine to start the GUI application.
- `detectors.FaceDetector`: A class for face detection.
    - `detect`: A method to detect faces in a grayscale image. Optionally, the image is downscaled for better reliability. Upon successful detection, the method returns the extracted head region.
    - `align_head`: A method to preprocess an extracted head region with affine transformations such that the resulting face appears centered and upright.
- `classifiers.Classifier`: An abstract base class that defines the common interface for all classifiers (same as in *Chapter 6, Learning to Recognize Traffic Signs*).
- `classifiers.MultiLayerPerceptron`: A class that implements an MLP by using the following public methods:
    - `fit`: A method to fit the MLP to the training data. It takes as input, a matrix of the training data, where each row is a training sample, and columns contain feature values, and a vector of labels.
    - `evaluate`: A method to evaluate the MLP by applying it to some test data after training. It takes as input, a matrix of test data, where each row is a test sample and columns contain feature values, and a vector of labels. The function returns three different performance metrics: accuracy, precision, and recall.

- ○ `predict`: A method to predict the class labels of some test data. We expose this method to the user so it can be applied to any number of data samples, which will be helpful in the testing mode, when we do not want to evaluate the entire dataset, but instead predict the label of only a single data sample.

  - ○ `save`: A method to save a trained MLP to file.

  - ○ `load`: A method to load a pre-trained MLP from file.

- ● `train_test_mlp`: A script to train and test an MLP by applying it to our self-recorded dataset. The script will explore different network architectures and store the one with the best generalization performance in a file, so that the pre-trained classifier can be loaded later.

- • `datasets.homebrew`: A class to parse the self-recorded training set. Analogously to the previous chapter, the class contains the following methods:

  - ○ `load_data`: A method to load the training set, perform PCA on it via the `extract_features` function, and split the data into the training and test sets. Optionally, the preprocessed data can be stored in a file so that we can load it later on without having to parse the data again.

  - ○ `load_from_file`: A method to load a previously stored preprocessed dataset.

  - ○ `extract_features`: A method to extract a feature of choice (in the present chapter: to perform PCA on the data). We expose this function to the user so it can be applied to any number of data samples, which will be helpful in the testing mode, when we do not want to parse the entire dataset but instead predict the label of only a single data sample.

- • `gui`: A module providing a wxPython GUI application to access the capture device and display the video feed. This is the same module that we used in the previous chapters.

  - ○ `gui.BaseLayout`: A generic layout from which more complicated layouts can be built. This chapter does not require any modifications to the basic layout.

In the following sections, we will discuss these components in detail.

Face detection

OpenCV comes preinstalled with a range of sophisticated classifiers for general-purpose object detection. Perhaps, the most commonly known detector is the **cascade of Haar-based feature detectors** for face detection, which was invented by Paul Viola and Michael Jones.

Haar-based cascade classifiers

Every book on OpenCV should at least mention the Viola–Jones face detector. Invented in 2001, this cascade classifier disrupted the field of computer vision, as it finally allowed real-time face detection and face recognition.

The classifier is based on Haar-like features (similar to Haar basis functions), which sum up the pixel intensities in small regions of an image, as well as capture the difference between adjacent image regions. Some example rectangle features are shown in the following figure, relative to the enclosing (light gray) detection window:

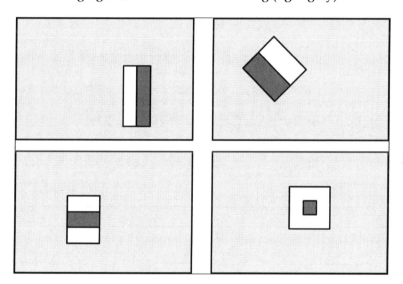

Here, the top row shows two examples of an edge feature, either vertically oriented (left) or oriented at a 45 degree angle (right). The bottom row shows a line feature (left) and a center-surround feature (right). The feature value for each of these is then calculated by summing up all pixel values in the dark gray rectangle and subtracting this value from the sum of all pixel values in the white rectangle. This procedure allowed the algorithm to capture certain qualities of human faces, such as the fact that eye regions are usually darker than the region surrounding the cheeks.

Thus, a common Haar feature would have a dark rectangle (representing the eye region) atop a bright rectangle (representing the cheek region). Combining this feature with a bank of rotated and slightly more complicated *wavelets*, Viola and Jones arrived at a powerful feature descriptor for human faces. In an additional act of genius, these guys came up with an efficient way to calculate these features, making it possible for the first time to detect faces in real-time.

Pre-trained cascade classifiers

Even better, this approach does not only work for faces but also for eyes, mouths, full bodies, company logos, you name it. A number of pre-trained classifiers can be found under the OpenCV install path in the data folder:

Cascade classifier type	XML file name
Face detector (default)	haarcascade_frontalface_default. xml
Face detector (fast Haar)	haarcascade_frontalface_alt2.xml
Eye detector	haarcascade_lefteye_2splits.xml
	haarcascade_righteye_2splits.xml
Mouth detector	haarcascade_mcs_mouth.xml
Nose detector	haarcascade_mcs_nose.xml
Full body detector	haarcascade_fullbody.xml

In this chapter, we will use haarcascade_frontalface_default.xml, haarcascade_lefteye_2splits.xml, and haarcascade_righteye_2splits.xml.

 If you are wearing glasses, make sure to use haarcascade_eye_ tree_eyeglasses.xml on both eyes instead.

Using a pre-trained cascade classifier

A cascade classifier can be loaded and applied to a (grayscale!) image frame with the following code:

```
import cv2

frame = cv2.imrcad('example_grayscale.jpg', cv2.CV_8UC1)
face_casc =
    cv2.CascadeClassifier('haarcascade_frontalface_default.xml')
faces = face_casc.detectMultiScale(frame, scaleFactor=1.1,
    minNeighbors=3)
```

The detectMultiScale function comes with a number of options:

- minFeatureSize: The minimum face size to consider (for example, 20 × 20 pixels).

- searchScaleFactor: Amount by which to rescale the image (scale pyramid). For example, a value of 1.1 will gradually reduce the size of the input image by 10 percent, making it more likely for a face to be found than a larger value.

- minNeighbors: The number of neighbors each candidate rectangle should have to retain it. Typically, choose 3 or 5.

- flags: Options for old cascades (will be ignored by newer ones). For example, whether to look for all faces or just the largest (cv2.cv.CASCADE_FIND_BIGGEST_OBJECT).

If detection is successful, the function will return a list of bounding boxes (faces) that contain the coordinates of the detected face regions:

```
for (x, y, w, h) in faces:
    # draw bounding box on frame
    cv2.rectangle(frame, (x, y), (x + w, y + h), (100, 255, 0), 2)
```

If your pre-trained face cascade does not detect anything, a common reason is usually that the path to the pre-trained cascade file could not be found. In this case, CascadeClassifier will fail silently. Thus, it is always a good idea to check whether the returned classifier casc = cv2.CascadeClassifier(filename) is empty, by checking casc.empty().

The FaceDetector class

All relevant face detection code for this chapter can be found as part of the FaceDetector class in the detectors module. Upon instantiation, this class loads three different cascade classifiers that are needed for preprocessing: a face cascade and two eye cascades.

```
import cv2
import numpy as np


class FaceDetector:
    def __init__(
```

```
self,
face_casc='params/haarcascade_frontalface_default.xml',
left_eye_casc='params/haarcascade_lefteye_2splits.xml',
right_eye_casc='params/haarcascade_righteye_2splits.xml',
scale_factor=4):
```

Because our preprocessing requires a valid face cascade, we make sure that the file can be loaded. If not, we print an error message and exit the program:

```
self.face_casc = cv2.CascadeClassifier(face_casc)
if self.face_casc.empty():
    print 'Warning: Could not load face cascade:',
        face_casc
    raise SystemExit
```

For reasons that will become clear in just a moment, we also need two eye cascades, for which we proceed analogously:

```
self.left_eye_casc = cv2.CascadeClassifier(left_eye_casc)
if self.left_eye_casc.empty():
    print 'Warning: Could not load left eye cascade:',
        left_eye_casc
    raise SystemExit
self.right_eye_casc =
    cv2.CascadeClassifier(right_eye_casc)
if self.right_eye_casc.empty():
    print 'Warning: Could not load right eye cascade:',
        right_eye_casc
    raise SystemExit
```

Face detection works best on low-resolution grayscale images. This is why we also store a scaling factor (`scale_factor`) so that we can operate on downscaled versions of the input image if necessary:

```
self.scale_factor = scale_factor
```

Detecting faces in grayscale images

Faces can then be detected using the `detect` method. Here, we ensure that we operate on a downscaled grayscale image:

```
def detect(self, frame):
    frameCasc = cv2.cvtColor(cv2.resize(frame, (0, 0),
        fx=1.0 / self.scale_factor, fy=1.0 / self.scale_factor),
        cv2.COLOR_RGB2GRAY)
    faces = self.face_casc.detectMultiScale(frameCasc,
        scaleFactor=1.1, minNeighbors=3,
        flags=cv2.cv.CV_HAAR_FIND_BIGGEST_OBJECT) *
        self.scale_factor
```

If a face is found, we continue to extract the head region from the bounding box information and store the result in `head`:

```
for (x, y, w, h) in faces:
    head = cv2.cvtColor(frame[y:y + h, x:x + w],
        cv2.COLOR_RGB2GRAY)
```

We also draw the bounding box onto the input image:

```
cv2.rectangle(frame, (x, y), (x + w, y + h), (100, 255, 0), 2)
```

In case of success, the method should return a Boolean indicating success (`True`), the annotated input image (`frame`), and the extracted head region (`head`):

```
return True, frame, head
```

Otherwise, if no faces were detected, the method indicates failure with a Boolean (`False`) and returns the unchanged input image (`frame`) and `None` for the head region:

```
return False, frame, None
```

Preprocessing detected faces

After a face has been detected, we might want to preprocess the extracted head region before applying classification on it. Although the face cascade is fairly accurate, for recognition, it is important that all the faces are upright and centered on the image. This idea is best illustrated with an image. Consider a sad programmer under a tree:

Because of his emotional state, the programmer tends to keep his head slightly tilted to the side while looking down. The facial region as extracted by the face cascade is shown as the leftmost grayscale thumbnail on the right. In order to compensate for the head orientation, we aim to rotate and scale the face so that all data samples will be perfectly aligned. This is the job of the `align_head` method in the `FaceDetector` class:

```
def align_head(self, head):
    height, width = head.shape[:2]
```

Fortunately, OpenCV comes with a few eye cascades that can detect both open and closed eyes, such as `haarcascade_lefteye_2splits.xml` and `haarcascade_righteye_2splits.xml`. This allows us to calculate the angle between the line that connects the center of the two eyes and the horizon so that we can rotate the face accordingly. In addition, adding eye detectors will reduce the risk of having false positives in our dataset, allowing us to add a data sample only if both the head and the eyes have been successfully detected.

After loading these eye cascades from file in the FaceDetector constructor, they are applied to the input image (head):

```
left_eye_region = head[0.2*height:0.5*height,
    0.1*width:0.5*width]
left_eye = self.left_eye_casc.detectMultiScale(
    left_eye_region, scaleFactor=1.1, minNeighbors=3,
    flags=cv2.cv.CV_HAAR_FIND_BIGGEST_OBJECT)
```

Here, it is important that we pass only a small, relevant region (`left_eye_region`; compare small thumbnails in the top-right corner of the preceding figure) to the eye cascades. For simplicity, we use hardcoded values that focus on the top half of the facial region and assume the left eye to be in the left half.

If an eye is detected, we extract the coordinates of its center point:

```
left_eye_center = None
for (xl, yl, wl, hl) in left_eye:
    # find the center of the detected eye region
    left_eye_center = np.array([0.1 * width + xl + wl / 2,
        0.2 * height + yl + hl / 2])
    break # need only look at first, largest eye
```

Then, we proceed to do the same for the right eye:

```
right_eye_region = head[0.2*height:0.5*height,
    0.5*width:0.9*width]
right_eye = self.right_eye_casc.detectMultiScale(
    right_eye_region, scaleFactor=1.1, minNeighbors=3,
    flags=cv2.cv.CV_HAAR_FIND_BIGGEST_OBJECT)
right_eye_center = None
for (xr, yr, wr, hr) in right_eye:
    # find the center of the detected eye region
    right_eye_center = np.array([0.5 * width + xr + wr / 2,
        0.2 * height + yr + hr / 2])
    break  # need only look at first, largest eye
```

As mentioned earlier, if we do not detect both the eyes, we discard the sample as a false positive:

```
if left_eye_center is None or right_eye_center is None:
    return False, head
```

Now, this is where the magic happens. No matter how crooked the face that we detected is, before we add it to the training set, we want the eyes to be exactly at 25 percent and 75 percent of the image width (so that the face is in the center) and at 20 percent of the image height:

```
desired_eye_x = 0.25
desired_eye_y = 0.2
desired_img_width = 200
desired_img_height = desired_img_width
```

This can be achieved by warping the image using cv2.warpAffine (remember *Chapter 3, Finding Objects via Feature Matching and Perspective Transforms?*). First, we calculate the angle (in degrees) between the line that connects the two eyes and a horizontal line:

```
eye_center = (left_eye_center + right_eye_center) / 2
eye_angle_deg = np.arctan2(
    right_eye_center[1] - left_eye_center[1],
    right_eye_center[0] - left_eye_center[0]) *
    180.0 / cv2.cv.CV_PI
```

Then, we derive a scaling factor that will scale the distance between the two eyes to be exactly 50 percent of the image width:

```
eye_size_scale = (1.0 - desired_eye_x * 2) *
    desired_img_width / np.linalg.norm(
    right_eye_center - left_eye_center)
```

With these two parameters (`eye_angle_deg` and `eye_size_scale`) in hand, we can now come up with a suitable rotation matrix that will transform our image:

```
rot_mat = cv2.getRotationMatrix2D(tuple(eye_center),
eye_angle_deg, eye_size_scale)
```

We make sure that the center of the eyes will be centered in the image:

```
rot_mat[0,2] += desired_img_width*0.5 - eye_center[0]
rot_mat[1,2] += desired_eye_y*desired_img_height -
    eye_center[1]
```

Finally, we arrive at an upright scaled version of the facial region that looks like the lower-right thumbnail of the preceding image:

```
res = cv2.warpAffine(head, rot_mat,
    (desired_img_width, desired_img_height))
return True, res
```

Facial expression recognition

The facial expression recognition pipeline is encapsulated by `chapter7.py`. This file consists of an interactive GUI that operates in two modes (training and testing), as described earlier.

In order to arrive at our end-to-end app, we need to cover the following three steps:

1. Load the `chapter7.py` GUI in the training mode to assemble a training set.

2. Train an MLP classifier on the training set via `train_test_mlp.py`. Because this step can take a long time, the process takes place in its own script. After successful training, store the trained weights in a file, so that we can load the pre-trained MLP in the next step.

3. Load the `chapter7.py` GUI in the testing mode to classify facial expressions on a live video stream in real-time. This step involves loading several pre-trained cascade classifiers as well as our pre-trained MLP classifier. These classifiers will then be applied to every captured video frame.

Assembling a training set

Before we can train an MLP, we need to assemble a suitable training set. Because chances are, that your face is not yet part of any dataset out there (the NSA's private collection doesn't count), we will have to assemble our own. This is done most easily by returning to our GUI application from the previous chapters, which can access a webcam, and operate on each frame of a video stream.

The GUI will present the user with the option of recording one of the following six emotional expressions: neutral, happy, sad, surprised, angry, and disgusted. Upon clicking a button, the app will take a snapshot of the detected facial region, and upon exiting, it will store all collected data samples in a file. These samples can then be loaded from file and used to train an MLP classifier in `train_test_mlp.py`, as described in step two given earlier.

Running the screen capture

In order to run this app (`chapter7.py`), we need to set up a screen capture by using `cv2.VideoCapture` and pass the handle to the `FaceLayout` class:

```
import time
import wx
from os import path
import cPickle as pickle

import cv2
import numpy as np

from datasets import homebrew
from detectors import FaceDetector
from classifiers import MultiLayerPerceptron
from gui import BaseLayout


def main():
    capture = cv2.VideoCapture(0)
    if not(capture.isOpened()):
        capture.open()

    capture.set(cv2.cv.CV_CAP_PROP_FRAME_WIDTH, 640)
    capture.set(cv2.cv.CV_CAP_PROP_FRAME_HEIGHT, 480)

    # start graphical user interface
    app = wx.App()
```

```
layout = FaceLayout(None, -1, 'Facial Expression Recognition',
    capture)
layout.init_algorithm()
layout.Show(True)
app.MainLoop()

if __name__ == '__main__':
    main()
```

If you happen to have installed some non-canonical releases of OpenCV, the frame width and frame weight parameters might have a slightly different name (for example, `cv3.CAP_PROP_FRAME_WIDTH`). However, in newer releases, it is the easiest to access the old OpenCV1 sub-module cv and its variables `cv2.cv.CV_CAP_PROP_FRAME_WIDTH` and `cv2.cv.CV_CAP_PROP_FRAME_HEIGHT`.

The GUI constructor

Analogous to the previous chapters, the GUI of the app is a customized version of the generic `BaseLayout`:

```
class FaceLayout(BaseLayout):
```

We initialize the training samples and labels as empty lists, and make sure to call the `_on_exit` method upon closing the window so that the training data is dumped to file:

```
def _init_custom_layout(self):
    # initialize data structure
    self.samples = []
    self.labels = []

    # call method to save data upon exiting
    self.Bind(wx.EVT_CLOSE, self._on_exit)
```

We also have to load several classifiers to make the preprocessing and (later on) the real-time classification work. For convenience, default file names are provided:

```
def init_algorithm(
    self,
    save_training_file='datasets/faces_training.pkl',
    load_preprocessed_data='datasets/faces_preprocessed.pkl',
    load_mlp='params/mlp.xml',
    face_casc='params/haarcascade_frontalface_default.xml',
    left_eye_casc='params/haarcascade_lefteye_2splits.xml',
    right_eye_casc='params/haarcascade_righteye_2splits.xml'):
```

Here, `save_training_file` indicates the name of a pickle file in which to store all
training samples after data acquisition is complete:

```
self.dataFile = save_training_file
```

The three cascades are passed to the `FaceDetector` class as explained in the
previous section:

```
self.faces = FaceDetector(face_casc, left_eye_casc,
    right_eye_casc)
```

As their names suggest, the remaining two arguments (`load_preprocessed_data`
and `load_mlp`) are concerned with a real-time classification of the detected faces by
using the pre-trained MLP classifier:

```
# load preprocessed dataset to access labels and PCA
# params
if path.isfile(load_preprocessed_data):
    (_, y_train), (_, y_test), self.pca_V, self.pca_m =
        homebrew.load_from_file(load_preprocessed_data)
    self.all_labels = np.unique(np.hstack((y_train,
        y_test)))

    # load pre-trained multi-layer perceptron
    if path.isfile(load_mlp):
        self.MLP = MultiLayerPerceptron(
            np.array([self.pca_V.shape[1],
            len(self.all_labels)]),
            self.all_labels)
        self.MLP.load(load_mlp)
```

If any of the parts required for the testing mode are missing, we print a warning
and disable the testing mode altogether:

```
    else:
        print "Warning: Testing is disabled"
        print "Could not find pre-trained MLP file ",
            load_mlp
        self.testing.Disable()
else:
    print "Warning: Testing is disabled"
    print "Could not find preprocessed data file ",
        loadPreprocessedData
self.testing.Disable()
```

The GUI layout

Creation of the layout is again deferred to a method called `_create_custom_layout`. We keep the layout as simple as possible: We create a panel for the acquired video frame, and draw a row of buttons below it.

The idea is to then click one of the six radio buttons to indicate which facial expression you are trying to record, then place your head within the bounding box, and click the `Take Snapshot` button.

Below the current camera frame, we place two radio buttons to select either the training or the testing mode, and tell the GUI that the two are mutually exclusive by specifying `style=wx.RB_GROUP`:

```
def _create_custom_layout(self):
    # create horizontal layout with train/test buttons
    pnl1 = wx.Panel(self, -1)
    self.training = wx.RadioButton(pnl1, -1, 'Train', (10, 10),
        style=wx.RB_GROUP)
    self.testing = wx.RadioButton(pnl1, -1, 'Test')
    hbox1 = wx.BoxSizer(wx.HORIZONTAL)
    hbox1.Add(self.training, 1)
    hbox1.Add(self.testing, 1)
    pnl1.SetSizer(hbox1)
```

Also, we want the event of a button click to bind to the `self._on_training` and `self._on_testing` methods, respectively:

```
self.Bind(wx.EVT_RADIOBUTTON, self._on_training,
    self.training)
self.Bind(wx.EVT_RADIOBUTTON, self._on_testing, self.testing)
```

The second row should contain similar arrangements for the six facial expression buttons:

```
# create a horizontal layout with all buttons
pnl2 = wx.Panel(self, -1 )
self.neutral = wx.RadioButton(pnl2, -1, 'neutral',
    (10, 10), style=wx.RB_GROUP)
self.happy = wx.RadioButton(pnl2, -1, 'happy')
self.sad = wx.RadioButton(pnl2, -1, 'sad')
self.surprised = wx.RadioButton(pnl2, -1, 'surprised')
self.angry = wx.RadioButton(pnl2, -1, 'angry')
self.disgusted = wx.RadioButton(pnl2, -1, 'disgusted')
hbox2 = wx.BoxSizer(wx.HORIZONTAL)
hbox2.Add(self.neutral, 1)
hbox2.Add(self.happy, 1)
```

```
hbox2.Add(self.sad, 1)
hbox2.Add(self.surprised, 1)
hbox2.Add(self.angry, 1)
hbox2.Add(self.disgusted, 1)
pnl2.SetSizer(hbox2)
```

The **Take Snapshot** button is placed below the radio buttons and will bind to the `_on_snapshot` method:

```
pnl3 = wx.Panel(self, -1)
self.snapshot = wx.Button(pnl3, -1, 'Take Snapshot')
self.Bind(wx.EVT_BUTTON, self.OnSnapshot, self.snapshot)
hbox3 = wx.BoxSizer(wx.HORIZONTAL)
hbox3.Add(self.snapshot, 1)
pnl3.SetSizer(hbox3)
```

This will look like the following:

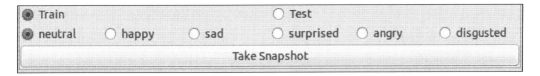

To make these changes take effect, the created panels need to be added to the list of existing panels:

```
# display the button layout beneath the video stream
self.panels_vertical.Add (pnl1, flag=wx.EXPAND | wx.TOP, border=1)
self.panels_vertical.Add(pnl2, flag=wx.EXPAND | wx.BOTTOM,
    border=1)
self.panels_vertical.Add(pnl3, flag=wx.EXPAND | wx.BOTTOM,
    border=1)
```

The rest of the visualization pipeline is handled by the `BaseLayout` class. Now, whenever the user clicks the `self.testing` button, we no longer want to record training samples, but instead switch to the testing mode. In the testing mode, none of the training-related buttons should be enabled, as shown in the following image:

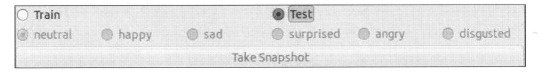

This can be achieved with the following method that disables all the relevant buttons:

```
def _on_testing(self, evt):
    """Whenever testing mode is selected, disable all
        training-related buttons"""
    self.neutral.Disable()
    self.happy.Disable()
    self.sad.Disable()
    self.surprised.Disable()
    self.angry.Disable()
    self.disgusted.Disable()
    self.snapshot.Disable()
```

Analogously, when we switch back to the training mode, the buttons should be enabled again:

```
def _on_training(self, evt):
    """Whenever training mode is selected, enable all
        training-related buttons"""
    self.neutral.Enable()
    self.happy.Enable()
    self.sad.Enable()
    self.surprised.Enable()
    self.angry.Enable()
    self.disgusted.Enable()
    self.snapshot.Enable()
```

Processing the current frame

The rest of the visualization pipeline is handled by the BaseLayout class. We only need to make sure to provide the _process_frame method. This method begins by detecting faces in a downscaled grayscale version of the current frame, as explained in the previous section:

```
def _process_frame(self, frame):
    success, frame, self.head = self.faces.detect(frame)
```

If a face is found, success is True, and the method has access to an annotated version of the current frame (frame) and the extracted head region (self.head). Note that we store the extracted head region for further reference, so that we can access it in _on_snapshot.

We will return to this method when we talk about the testing mode, but for now, this is all we need to know. Don't forget to pass the processed frame:

```
    return frame
```

Adding a training sample to the training set

When the Take Snapshot button is clicked upon, the _on_snapshot method is called. This method detects the emotional expression that we are trying to record by checking the value of all radio buttons, and assigns a class label accordingly:

```python
def _on_snapshot(self, evt):
    if self.neutral.GetValue():
        label = 'neutral'
    elif self.happy.GetValue():
        label = 'happy'
    elif self.sad.GetValue():
        label = 'sad'
    elif self.surprised.GetValue():
        label = 'surprised'
    elif self.angry.GetValue():
        label = 'angry'
    elif self.disgusted.GetValue():
        label = 'disgusted'
```

We next need to look at the detected facial region of the current frame (stored in self.head by _process_frame), and align it with all the other collected frames. That is, we want all the faces to be upright and the eyes to be aligned. Otherwise, if we do not align the data samples, we run the risk of having the classifier compare eyes to noses. Because this computation can be costly, we do not apply it on every frame, but instead only upon taking a snapshot. The alignment takes place in the following method:

```python
    if self.head is None:
        print "No face detected"
    else:
        success, head = self.faces.align_head(self.head)
```

If this method returns True for success, indicating that the sample was successfully aligned with all other samples, we add the sample to our dataset:

```python
    if success:
        print "Added sample to training set"
        self.samples.append(head.flatten())
        self.labels.append(label)
    else:
        print "Could not align head (eye detection failed?)"
```

All that is left to do now is to make sure that we save the training set upon exiting.

Dumping the complete training set to a file

Upon exiting the app (for example, by clicking the **Close** button of the window), an event EVT_CLOSE is triggered, which binds to the _on_exit method. This method simply dumps the collected samples and the corresponding class labels to file:

```
def _on_exit(self, evt):
    """Called whenever window is closed"""
    # if we have collected some samples, dump them to file
    if len(self.samples) > 0:
```

However, we want to make sure that we do not accidentally overwrite previously stored training sets. If the provided filename already exists, we append a suffix and save the data to the new filename instead:

```
# make sure we don't overwrite an existing file
if path.isfile(self.data_file):
    filename, fileext = path.splitext(self.data_file)
    offset = 0
    while True: # a do while loop
        file = filename + "-" + str(offset) + fileext
        if path.isfile(file):
            offset += 1
        else:
            break
    self.data_file = file
```

Once we have created an unused filename, we dump the data to file by making use of the pickle module:

```
f = open(self.dataFile, 'wb')
pickle.dump(self.samples, f)
pickle.dump(self.labels, f)
f.close()
```

Upon exiting, we inform the user that a file was created and make sure that all data structures are correctly deallocated:

```
print "Saved", len(self.samples), "samples to", self.data_file
self.Destroy()
```

Here are some examples from the assembled training set I:

| neutral | happy | sad | surprised | angry | disgusted |

Feature extraction

We have previously made the point that, finding the features that best describe the data is often an essential part of the entire learning task. We have also looked at common preprocessing methods such as **mean subtraction** and **normalization**. Here, we will look at an additional method that has a long tradition in face recognition: **principal component analysis (PCA)**.

Preprocessing the dataset

Analogous to *Chapter 6, Learning to Recognize Traffic Signs*, we write a new dataset parser in dataset/homebrew.py that will parse our self-assembled training set. We define a load_data function that will parse the dataset, perform feature extraction, split the data into training and testing sets, and return the results:

```
import cv2
import numpy as np

import csv
from matplotlib import cm
from matplotlib import pyplot as plt

from os import path
```

```
import cPickle as pickle


def load_data(load_from_file, test_split=0.2, num_components=50,
    save_to_file=None, plot_samples=False, seed=113):
    """load dataset from pickle """
```

Here, `load_from_file` specifies the path to the data file that we created in the previous section. We can also specify another file called `save_to_file`, which will contain the dataset after feature extraction. This will be helpful later on when we perform real-time classification.

The first step is thus to try and open `load_from_file`. If the file exists, we use the pickle module to load the `samples` and `labels` data structures; else, we throw an error:

```
# prepare lists for samples and labels
X = []
labels = []
if not path.isfile(load_from_file):
    print "Could not find file", load_from_file
    return (X, labels), (X, labels), None, None
else:
    print "Loading data from", load_from_file
    f = open(load_from_file, 'rb')
    samples = pickle.load(f)
    labels = pickle.load(f)
    print "Loaded", len(samples), "training samples"
```

If the file was successfully loaded, we perform PCA on all samples. The `num_components` variable specifies the number of principal components that we want to consider. The function also returns a list of basis vectors (V) and a mean value (m) for every sample in the set:

```
# perform feature extraction
# returns preprocessed samples, PCA basis vectors & mean
X, V, m = extract_features(samples,
    num_components=num_components)
```

As pointed out earlier, it is imperative to keep the samples that we use to train our classifier separate from the samples that we use to test it. For this, we shuffle the data and split it into two separate sets, such that the training set contains a fraction (1 - `test_split`) of all samples, and the rest of the samples belong to the test set:

```
# shuffle dataset
np.random.seed(seed)
np.random.shuffle(X)
```

```
np.random.seed(seed)
np.random.shuffle(labels)

# split data according to test_split
X_train = X[:int(len(X)*(1-test_split))]
y_train = labels[:int(len(X)*(1-test_split))]

X_test = X[int(len(X)*(1-test_split)):]
y_test = labels[int(len(X)*(1-test_split)):]
```

If specified, we want to save the preprocessed data to file:

```
if save_to_file is not None:
    # dump all relevant data structures to file
    f = open(save_to_file, 'wb')
    pickle.dump(X_train, f)
    pickle.dump(y_train, f)
    pickle.dump(X_test, f)
    pickle.dump(y_test, f)
    pickle.dump(V, f)
    pickle.dump(m, f)
    f.close()
    print "Save preprocessed data to", save_to_file
```

Finally, we can return the extracted data:

```
return (X_train, y_train), (X_test, y_test), V, m
```

Principal component analysis

PCA is a dimensionality reduction technique that is helpful whenever we are dealing with high-dimensional data. In a sense, you can think of an image as a point in a high-dimensional space. If we flatten a 2D image of height m and width n (by concatenating either all rows or all columns), we get a (feature) vector of length m × n. The value of the i-th element in this vector is the grayscale value of the i-th pixel in the image. To describe every possible 2D grayscale image with these exact dimensions, we will need an m × n dimensional vector space that contains 256 raised to the power of m × n vectors. Wow! An interesting question that comes to mind when considering these numbers is as follows: could there be a smaller, more compact vector space (using less than m × n features) that describes all these images equally well? After all, we have previously realized that grayscale values are not the most informative measures of content.

This is where PCA comes in. Consider a dataset from which we extracted exactly two features. These features could be the grayscale values of pixels at some x and y positions, but they could also be more complex than that. If we plot the dataset along these two feature axes, the data might lie within some multivariate Gaussian, as shown in the following image:

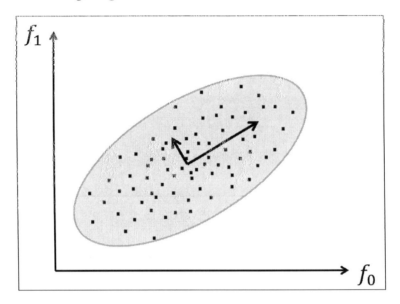

What PCA does is *rotate* all data points until the data lie aligned with the two *axes* (the two inset vectors) that explain most of the *spread* of the data. PCA considers these two axes to be the most informative, because if you walk along them, you can see most of the data points separated. In more technical terms, PCA aims to transform the data to a new coordinate system by means of an orthogonal linear transformation. The new coordinate system is chosen such that if you project the data onto these new axes, the first coordinate (called the **first principal component**) observes the greatest variance. In the preceding image, the small vectors drawn correspond to the eigenvectors of the covariance matrix, shifted so that their tails come to lie at the mean of the distribution.

Fortunately, someone else has already figured out how to do all this in Python. In OpenCV, performing PCA is as simple as calling `cv2.PCACompute`. Embedded in our feature extraction method, the option reads as follows:

```
def extract_feature(X, V=None, m=None, num_components=50):
```

Here, the function can be used to either perform PCA from scratch or use a previously calculated set of basis vectors (V) and mean (m), which is helpful during testing when we want to perform real-time classification. The number of principal components to consider is specified via num_components. If we do not specify any of the optional arguments, PCA is performed from scratch on all the data samples in X:

```
if V is None or m is None:
    # need to perform PCA from scratch
    if num_components is None:
        num_components = 50

    # cols are pixels, rows are frames
    Xarr = np.squeeze(np.array(X).astype(np.float32))

    # perform PCA, returns mean and basis vectors
    m, V = cv2.PCACompute(Xarr)
```

The beauty of PCA is that the first principal component by definition explains most of the variance of the data. In other words, the first principal component is the most informative of the data. This means that we do not need to keep all of the components to get a good representation of the data! We can limit ourselves to the num_components most informative ones:

```
# use only the first num_components principal components
V = V[:num_components]
```

Finally, a compressed representation of the data is achieved by projecting the zero-centered original data onto the new coordinate system:

```
for i in xrange(len(X)):
    X[i] = np.dot(V, X[i] - m[0, i])

return X, V, m
```

Multi-layer perceptrons

Multi-layer perceptrons (MLPs) have been around for a while. MLPs are artificial neural networks (ANNs) used to convert a set of input data into a set of output data. At the heart of an MLP is a **perceptron**, which resembles (yet overly simplifies) a biological neuron. By combining a large number of perceptrons in multiple layers, the MLP is able to make non-linear decisions about its input data. Furthermore, MLPs can be trained with **backpropagation**, which makes them very interesting for supervised learning.

The perceptron

A perceptron is a binary classifier that was invented in the 1950s by Frank Rosenblatt. A perceptron calculates a weighted sum of its inputs, and if this sum exceeds a threshold, it outputs a 1; else, it outputs a 0. In some sense, a perceptron is integrating evidence that its afferents signal the presence (or absence) of some object instance, and if this evidence is strong enough, the perceptron will be active (or silent). This is loosely connected to what researchers believe biological neurons are doing (or can be used to do) in the brain, hence, the term artificial neural network.

A sketch of a perceptron is depicted in the following figure:

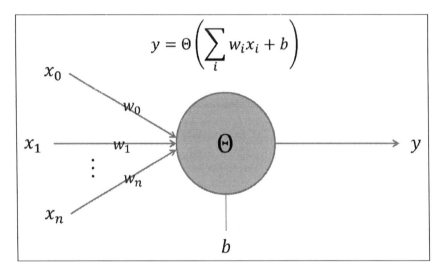

Here, a perceptron computes a weighted (w_i) sum of all its inputs (x_i), combined with a bias term (b). This input is fed into a nonlinear activation function (Θ) that determines the output of the perceptron (y). In the original algorithm, the activation function was the Heaviside step function. In modern implementations of ANNs, the activation function can be anything ranging from sigmoid to hyperbolic tangent functions. The Heaviside function and the sigmoid function are plotted in the following image:

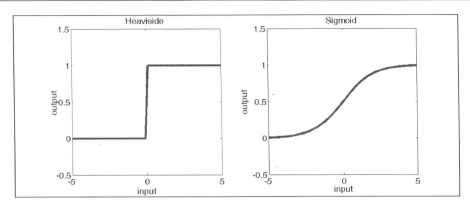

Depending on the activation function, these networks might be able to perform either classification or regression. Traditionally, one only talks of MLPs when nodes use the Heaviside step function.

Deep architectures

Once you have the perceptron figured out, it would make sense to combine multiple perceptrons to form a larger network. Multi-layer perceptrons usually consist of at least three layers, where the first layer has a node (or neuron) for every input feature of the dataset, and the last layer has a node for every class label. The layer in between is called the **hidden layer**. An example of this **feed-forward neural network** is shown in the following figure:

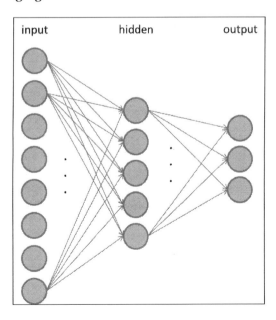

In a feed-forward neural network, some or all of the nodes in the input layer are connected to all the nodes in the hidden layer, and some or all of the nodes in the hidden layer are connected to some or all of the nodes in the output layer. You would usually choose the number of nodes in the input layer to be equal to the number of features in the dataset, so that each node represents one feature. Analogously, the number of nodes in the output layer is usually equal to the number of classes in the data, so that when an input sample of class c is presented, the c-th node in the output layer is active and all others are silent.

It is also possible to have multiple hidden layers of course. Often, it is not clear beforehand what the optimal size of the network should be.

Typically, you will see the error rate on the training set decrease when you add more neurons to the network, as is depicted in the following figure (thinner, red curve):

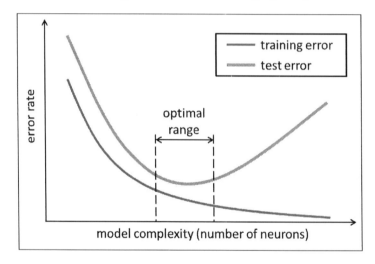

This is because the expressive power or complexity (also referred to as the **Vapnik–Chervonenkis** or **VC dimension**) of the model increases with the increasing size of the neural network. However, the same cannot be said for the error rate on the test set (thicker, blue curve)! Instead, what you will find is that with increasing model complexity, the test error goes through a minimum, and adding more neurons to the network will not improve the generalization performance any more. Therefore, you would want to steer the size of the neural network to what is labeled the optimal range in the preceding figure, which is where the network achieves the best generalization performance.

You can think of it this way. A model of weak complexity (on the far left of the plot) is probably too small to really understand the dataset that it is trying to learn, thus yielding large error rates on both the training and the test sets. This is commonly referred to as **underfitting**. On the other hand, a model on the far right of the plot is probably so complex that it begins to memorize the specifics of each sample in the training data, without paying attention to the general attributes that make a sample stand apart from the others. Therefore, the model will fail when it has to predict data that it is has never seen before, effectively yielding a large error rate on the test set. This is commonly referred to as **overfitting**.

Instead, what you want is to develop a model that neither underfits nor overfits. Often this can only be achieved by trial-and-error; that is, by considering the network size as a hyperparameter that needs to be tweaked and tuned depending on the exact task to be performed.

An MLP learns by adjusting its weights so that when an input sample of class c is presented, the c-th node in the output layer is active and all the others are silent. MLPs are trained by means of **backpropagation**, which is an algorithm to calculate the partial derivative of a **loss function** with respect to any synaptic weight or neuron bias in the network. These partial derivatives can then be used to update the weights and biases in the network in order to reduce the overall loss step-by-step.

A loss function can be obtained by presenting training samples to the network and by observing the network's output. By observing which output nodes are active and which are silent, we can calculate the relative error between what the output layer is doing and what it should be doing (that is, the loss function). We then make corrections to all the weights in the network so that the error decreases over time. It turns out that the error in the hidden layer depends on the output layer, and the error in the input layer depends on the error in both the hidden layer and the output layer. Thus, in a sense, the error (back)propagates through the network. In OpenCV, backpropagation is used by specifying `cv3.ANN_MLP_TRAIN_PARAMS_BACKPROP` in the training parameters.

> Gradient descent comes in two common flavors: In **stochastic gradient descent**, we update the weights after each presentation of a training example, whereas in **batch learning**, we present training examples in batches and update the weights only after each batch is presented. In both scenarios, we have to make sure that we adjust the weights only slightly per sample (by adjusting the **learning rate**) so that the network slowly converges to a stable solution over time.

An MLP for facial expression recognition

Analogous to *Chapter 6*, *Learning to Recognize Traffic Signs*, we will develop a multi-layer perceptron class that is modeled after the classifier base class. The base classifier contains a method for training, where a model is fitted to the training data, and for testing, where the trained model is evaluated by applying it to the test data:

```python
from abc import ABCMeta, abstractmethod

class Classifier:
    """Abstract base class for all classifiers"""
    __metaclass__ = ABCMeta

    @abstractmethod
    def fit(self, X_train, y_train):
        pass

    @abstractmethod
    def evaluate(self, X_test, y_test, visualize=False):
        pass
```

Here, X_train and X_test correspond to the training and the test data, respectively, where each row represents a sample and each column is a feature value of this sample. The training and test labels are passed as the y_train and y_test vectors, respectively.

We thus define a new class, MultiLayerPerceptron, which derives from the classifier base class:

```python
class MultiLayerPerceptron(Classifier):
```

The constructor of this class accepts an array called layer_sizes that specifies the number of neurons in each layer of the network and an array called class_labels that spells out all available class labels. The first layer will contain a neuron for each feature in the input, whereas the last layer will contain a neuron per output class:

```python
def __init__(self, layer_sizes, class_labels, params=None):
    self.num_features = layer_sizes[0]
    self.num_classes = layer_sizes[-1]
    self.class_labels = class_labels
    self.params = params or dict()
```

The constructor initializes the multi-layer perceptron by means of an OpenCV module called cv2.ANN_MLP:

```python
self.model = cv2.ANN_MLP()
self.model.create(layer_sizes)
```

For the sake of convenience to the user, the MLP class allows operations on string labels as enumerated via `class_labels` (for example, *neutral*, *happy*, and *sad*). Under the hood, the class will convert back and forth from strings to integers and from integers to strings, so that `cv2.ANN_MLP` will only be exposed to integers. These transformations are handled by the following two private methods:

```
def _labels_str_to_num(self, labels):
    """ convert string labels to their corresponding ints """
    return np.array([int(np.where(self.class_labels == l)[0])
        for l in labels])

def _labels_num_to_str(self, labels):
    """Convert integer labels to their corresponding string
        names """
    return self.class_labels[labels]
```

Load and save methods provide simple wrappers for the underlying `cv2.ANN_MLP` class:

```
def load(self, file):
    """ load a pre-trained MLP from file """
    self.model.load(file)

def save(self, file):
    """ save a trained MLP to file """
    self.model.save(file)
```

Training the MLP

Following the requirements defined by the `Classifier` base class, we need to perform training in a `fit` method:

```
def fit(self, X_train, y_train, params=None):
    """ fit model to data """
    if params is None:
        params = self.params
```

Here, `params` is an optional dictionary that contains a number of options relevant to training, such as the termination criteria (`term_crit`) and the learning algorithm (`train_method`) to be used during training. For example, to use backpropagation and terminate training either after 300 iterations or when the loss reaches values smaller than 0.01, specify `params` as follows:

```
params = dict(
    term_crit = (cv2.TERM_CRITERIA_COUNT, 300, 0.01),
    train_method = cv2.ANN_MLP_TRAIN_PARAMS_BACKPROP)
```

Because the `train` method of the `cv2.ANN_MLP` module does not allow integer-valued class labels, we need to first convert `y_train` into "one-hot" code, consisting only of zeros and ones, which can then be fed to the `train` method:

```
y_train = self._labels_str_to_num(y_train)
y_train = self._one_hot(y_train).reshape(-1,
    self.num_classes)
    self.model.train(X_train, y_train, None, params=params)
```

The one-hot code is taken care of in `_one_hot`:

```
def _one_hot(self, y_train):
    """Convert a list of labels into one-hot code """
```

Each class label c in `y_train` needs to be converted into a `self.num_classes`-long vector of zeros and ones, where all entries are zeros except the c-th, which is a one. We prepare this operation by allocating a vector of zeros:

```
num_samples = len(y_train)
new_responses = np.zeros(num_samples * self.num_classes,
    np.float32)
```

Then, we identify the indices of the vector that correspond to all the c-th class labels:

```
resp_idx = np.int32(y_train +
    np.arange(num_samples)  self.num_classes)
```

The vector elements at these indices then need to be set to one:

```
new_responses[resp_idx] = 1
return new_responses
```

Testing the MLP

Following the requirements defined by the `Classifier` base class, we need to perform training in an `evaluate` method:

```
def evaluate(self, X_test, y_test, visualize=False):
    """ evaluate model performance """
```

Analogous to the previous chapter, we will evaluate the performance of our classifier in terms of accuracy, precision, and recall. To reuse our previous code, we again need to come up with a 2D voting matrix, where each row stands for a data sample in the testing set and the c-th column contains the number of votes for the c-th class.

In the world of perceptrons, the voting matrix actually has a straightforward interpretation: The higher the activity of the c-th neuron in the output layer, the stronger the vote for the c-th class. So, all we need to do is to read out the activity of the output layer and plug it into our accuracy method:

```
ret, Y_vote = self.model.predict(X_test)
y_test = self._labels_str_to_num(y_test)
accuracy = self._accuracy(y_test, Y_vote)
precision = self._precision(y_test, Y_vote)
recall = self._recall(y_test, Y_vote)

return (accuracy, precision, recall)
```

In addition, we expose the predict method to the user, so that it is possible to predict the label of even a single data sample. This will be helpful when we perform real-time classification, where we do not want to iterate over all test samples, but instead only consider the current frame. This method simply predicts the label of an arbitrary number of samples and returns the class label as a human-readable string:

```
def predict(self, X_test):
    """ predict the labels of test data """
    ret, Y_vote = self.model.predict(X_test)

    # find the most active cell in the output layer
    y_hat = np.argmax(Y_vote, 1)

    # return string labels
    return self._labels_num_to_str(y_hat)
```

Running the script

The MLP classifier can be trained and tested by using the train_test_mlp.py script. The script first parses the homebrew dataset and extracts all class labels:

```
import cv2
import numpy as np

from datasets import homebrew
from classifiers import MultiLayerPerceptron

def main():
    # load training data
    # training data can be recorded using chapter7.py in training
    # mode
    (X_train, y_train),(X_test, y_test) =
```

```
        homebrew.load_data("datasets/faces_training.pkl",
            num_components=50, test_split=0.2,
            save_to_file="datasets/faces_preprocessed.pkl",
            seed=42)
    if len(X_train) == 0 or len(X_test) == 0:
        print "Empty data"
    raise SystemExit

    # convert to numpy
    X_train = np.squeeze(np.array(X_train)).astype(np.float32)
    y_train = np.array(y_train)
    X_test = np.squeeze(np.array(X_test)).astype(np.float32)
    y_test = np.array(y_test)

    # find all class labels
    labels = np.unique(np.hstack((y_train, y_test)))
```

We also make sure to provide some valid termination criteria as described above:

```
    params = dict( term_crit = (cv2.TERM_CRITERIA_COUNT, 300,
        0.01), train_method=cv2.ANN_MLP_TRAIN_PARAMS_BACKPROP,
        bp_dw_scale=0.001, bp_moment_scale=0.9 )
```

Often, the optimal size of the neural network is not known a priori, but instead, a hyperparameter needs to be tuned. In the end, we want the network that gives us the best generalization performance (that is, the network with the best accuracy measure on the test set). Since we do not know the answer, we will run a number of different-sized MLPs in a loop and store the best in a file called `saveFile`:

```
    save_file = 'params/mlp.xml'
    num_features = len(X_train[0])
    num_classes = len(labels)

    # find best MLP configuration
    print "1-hidden layer networks"
    best_acc = 0.0 # keep track of best accuracy
    for l1 in xrange(10):
        # gradually increase the hidden-layer size
        layer_sizes = np.int32([num_features,
            (l1 + 1) * num_features / 5,
            num_classes])
    MLP = MultiLayerPerceptron(layer_sizes, labels)
    print layer_sizes
```

The MLP is trained on `X_train` and tested on `X_test`:

```
MLP.fit(X_train, y_train, params=params)
(acc, _, _) = MLP.evaluate(X_train, y_train)
print " - train acc = ", acc
(acc, _, _) = MLP.evaluate(X_test, y_test)
print " - test acc = ", acc
```

Finally, the best MLP is saved to file:

```
if acc > best_acc:
    # save best MLP configuration to file
    MLP.save(saveFile)
best_acc = acc
```

The saved `params/mlp.xml` file that contains the network configuration and learned weights can then be loaded into the main GUI application (`chapter7.py`) by passing `loadMLP='params/mlp.xml'` to the `init_algorithm` method of the `FaceLayout` class. The default arguments throughout this chapter will make sure that everything works straight out of the box.

Putting it all together

In order to run our app, we will need to execute the main function routine (in `chapter7.py`) that loads the pre-trained cascade classifier and the pre-trained multi-layer perceptron, and applies them to each frame of the webcam live stream.

However, this time, instead of collecting more training samples, we will select the radio button that says **Test**. This will trigger an `EVT_RADIOBUTTON` event, which binds to `FaceLayout._on_testing`, disabling all training-related buttons in the GUI and switching the app to the testing mode. In this mode, the pre-trained MLP classifier is applied to every frame of the live stream, trying to predict the current facial expression.

As promised earlier, we now return to `FaceLayout._process_frame`:

```
def _process_frame(self, frame):
    """ detects face, predicts face label in testing mode """
```

Unchanged from what we discussed earlier, the method begins by detecting faces in a downscaled grayscale version of the current frame:

```
success, frame, self.head = self.faces.detect(frame)
```

However, in the testing mode, there is more to the function:

```
# in testing mode: predict label of facial expression
if success and self.testing.GetValue():
```

In order to apply our pre-trained MLP classifier to the current frame, we need to apply the same preprocessing to the current frame as we did with the entire training set. After aligning the head region, we apply PCA by using the pre-loaded basis vectors (self.pca_V) and mean values (self.pca_m):

```
# if face found: preprocess (align)
success, head = self.faces.align_head(self.head)
if success:
    # extract features using PCA (loaded from file)
    X, _, _ = homebrew.extract_features(
        [head.flatten()], self.pca_V, self.pca_m)
```

Then, we are ready to predict the class label of the current frame:

```
# predict label with pre-trained MLP
label = self.MLP.predict(np.array(X))[0]
```

Since the predict method already returns a string label, all that is left to do is to display it above the bounding box in the current frame:

```
# draw label above bounding box
cv2.putText(frame, str(label), (x,y-20),
    cv2.FONT_HERSHEY_COMPLEX, 1, (0,255,0), 2)
break # need only look at first, largest face
```

Finally, we are done!

```
return frame
```

The end result looks like the following:

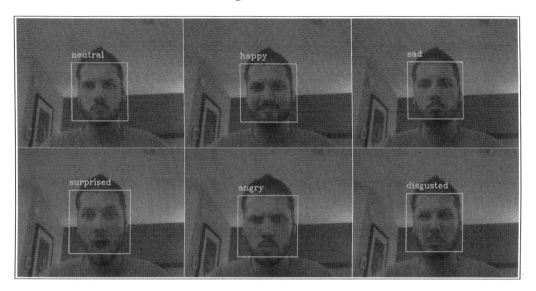

Although the classifier has only been trained on (roughly) 100 training samples, it reliably detects my various facial expressions in every frame of the live stream, no matter how distorted my face seemed to be at the moment. This is a good indication that the neural network that was learned neither underfits nor overfits the data, since it is capable of predicting the correct class labels even for new data samples.

Summary

The final chapter of this book has really rounded up our experience and made us combine a variety of our skills to arrive at an end-to-end app that consists of both object detection and object recognition. We became familiar with a range of pre-trained cascade classifiers that OpenCV has to offer, collected our very own training dataset, learned about multi-layer perceptrons, and trained them to recognize emotional expressions in faces. Well, at least my face.

The classifier was undoubtedly able to benefit from the fact that I was the only subject in the dataset, but with all the knowledge and experience that you have gathered with this book, it is now time to overcome these limitations! You can start small and train the classifier on images of you indoors and outdoors, at night and day, during summer and winter. Or, maybe, you are anxious to tackle a real-world dataset and be part of Kaggle's Facial Expression Recognition challenge (see `https://www.kaggle.com/c/challenges-in-representation-learning-facial-expression-recognition-challenge`).

If you are into machine learning, you might already know that there is a variety of accessible libraries out there, such as pylearn (https://github.com/lisa-lab/pylearn2), scikit-learn (http://scikit-learn.org), and pycaffe (http://caffe.berkeleyvision.org). Deep learning enthusiasts might want to look into Theano (http://deeplearning.net/software/theano) or Torch (http://torch.ch). Finally, if you find yourself stuck with all these algorithms and no datasets to apply them to, make sure to stop by the UC Irvine Machine Learning Repository (http://archive.ics.uci.edu/ml).

Congratulations! You are now an OpenCV expert.

Index

Symbols

3D point cloud visualization 73, 97-99
_create_custom_layout method 22
_init_base_layout method 20
_init_custom_layout method 22
_process_frame method 52

A

abstract base class (ABC) 19, 135
accuracy 129, 153
adaptive thresholding 1, 13
affine transformations 164
Alfheim dataset
  URL 122
app
  custom filter layout 22, 23
  FeatureMatching GUI 52
  GUI base class 18, 19
  implementing 127, 157-161, 197-199
  Kinect depth sensor, accessing 28, 29
  Kinect GUI 30, 31
  modules 74
  planning 50, 73, 104, 131
  prerequisites 104
  running 17, 18, 29, 51
  scripts 74
  setting up 27, 51
  summarizing 17, 18
  tasks performed 48-50
app setup
  about 82, 104
  main function routine 83, 84, 105, 106
  MultiObjectTracker class 106, 107

Saliency class 106
SceneReconstruction3D class 84, 85

B

backpropagation 187, 191
base class 135
BaseLayout class 22
batch learning 191
bilateral filter
  about 1, 13
  used, for edge-aware smoothing 13, 14
Binary Robust Independent Elementary
      Features (BRIEF) 56
black-and-white pencil sketch
  about 1
  creating 3
  dodging, in OpenCV 4-6
  pencil sketch transformation 6, 7
bookkeeping
  setting up, for mean-shift tracking 124, 125
bounding boxes
  extracting, for proto-objects 124
burning 1, 3

C

camera calibration
  about 71-76
  intrinsic camera parameters,
      estimating 76, 77
  pinhole camera model 75, 76
camera matrices
  finding 91-93
camera motion
  estimating, from pair of images 85, 86

Thank you for buying
OpenCV with Python Blueprints

About Packt Publishing

Packt, pronounced 'packed', published its first book, *Mastering phpMyAdmin for Effective MySQL Management*, in April 2004, and subsequently continued to specialize in publishing highly focused books on specific technologies and solutions.

Our books and publications share the experiences of your fellow IT professionals in adapting and customizing today's systems, applications, and frameworks. Our solution-based books give you the knowledge and power to customize the software and technologies you're using to get the job done. Packt books are more specific and less general than the IT books you have seen in the past. Our unique business model allows us to bring you more focused information, giving you more of what you need to know, and less of what you don't.

Packt is a modern yet unique publishing company that focuses on producing quality, cutting-edge books for communities of developers, administrators, and newbies alike. For more information, please visit our website at www.packtpub.com.

About Packt Open Source

In 2010, Packt launched two new brands, Packt Open Source and Packt Enterprise, in order to continue its focus on specialization. This book is part of the Packt Open Source brand, home to books published on software built around open source licenses, and offering information to anybody from advanced developers to budding web designers. The Open Source brand also runs Packt's Open Source Royalty Scheme, by which Packt gives a royalty to each open source project about whose software a book is sold.

Writing for Packt

We welcome all inquiries from people who are interested in authoring. Book proposals should be sent to author@packtpub.com. If your book idea is still at an early stage and you would like to discuss it first before writing a formal book proposal, then please contact us; one of our commissioning editors will get in touch with you.

We're not just looking for published authors; if you have strong technical skills but no writing experience, our experienced editors can help you develop a writing career, or simply get some additional reward for your expertise.

Instant OpenCV Starter

ISBN: 978-1-78216-881-2   Paperback: 56 pages

Get started with OpenCV using practical, hands-on projects

1. Learn something new in an Instant! A short, fast, focused guide delivering immediate results.

2. Step by step installation of OpenCV in Windows and Linux.

3. Examples and code based on real-life implementation of OpenCV to help the reader understand the importance of this technology.

4. Codes and algorithms with detailed explanations.

OpenCV Computer Vision with Python

ISBN: 978-1-78216-392-3   Paperback: 122 pages

Learn to capture videos, manipulate images, and track objects with Python using the OpenCV Library

1. Set up OpenCV, its Python bindings, and optional Kinect drivers on Windows, Mac or Ubuntu.

2. Create an application that tracks and manipulates faces.

3. Identify face regions using normal color images and depth images.

Please check **www.PacktPub.com** for information on our titles

OpenCV Essentials

ISBN: 978-1-78398-424-4   Paperback: 214 pages

Acquire, process, and analyze visual content to build full-fledged imaging applications using OpenCV

1. Create OpenCV programs with a rich user interface.

2. Develop real-world imaging applications using free tools and libraries.

3. Understand the intricate details of OpenCV and its implementation using easy-to-follow examples.

OpenCV Computer Vision Application Programming [Video]

ISBN: 978-1-84969-488-9   Duration: 02:27 hours

Incorporate OpenCV's powerful computer vision application programming techniques to build and make your own applications stand out from the crowd

1. Learn everything you need to get started with OpenCV.

2. Contains many practical examples covering different areas of computer vision that can be mixed and matched to build your own application.

3. Packed with code with relevant explanation to demonstrate real results from real images.

Please check **www.PacktPub.com** for information on our titles

Made in the USA
San Bernardino, CA
19 June 2016